BELI

AND

BROTHERHOOD

First published 2010

ISBN 978 0 85318 277 1

Published by Lewis Masonic

an imprint of Ian Allan Publishing Ltd, Hersham, Surrey KT12 4RG.
Printed by Ian Allan Printing Ltd, Hersham, Surrey KT12 4RG.

Visit the Ian Allan Publishing website at www.ianallanpublishing.com

Distributed in the United States of America and Canada by BookMasters Distribution Services.

CONTENTS

FOREWORD

I remember being at the back of a procession with an Episcopal colleague at a service in a packed Lancashire church. As we moved towards the west end, and before turning into the centre aisle, my colleague noticed a solid phalanx of men in the last pews on either side of the church. "What a fine body of men," he said in a voice that could not easily be missed by the people around. "Yes, indeed," I replied, "and they are all Freemasons."

The Bishop looked shaken. He was proposing to make a speech in the General Synod when the matter of Christians in Freemasonry was once again up for discussion. He was kind enough to ask, after the service, if I would be willing to discuss this with him. He admitted that his thinking was coloured by hearsay, information about which he could not be certain, and a good deal of prejudice occasioned by the notion of Masonic secrecy.

Would that this present book could have been available then to my Episcopal friend.

I believe it tackles head-on some of the critical issues in the debate about the compatibility of Christianity with Freemasonry.

It will appeal to those Masons who still find these questions cropping up in social, family, or church circles. It will perhaps reassure those Masons who, having resigned from their lodges during the turmoil of debates in the 1960s–1980s, miss their Masonry and would like to come back to it.

It will surely enlighten and delight the brother who is prepared to sit at the feet of someone who knows his Masonry, its origins, and the nuances of its workings through and through.

The Reverend Neville Barker Cryer writes with sincerity and conviction. The reader will discover both the breadth of his theological understanding and the depth of his Christian faith, and for good measure he will benefit from the fruits of the author's long researches into Freemasonry.

✠ *David Galliford, former Bishop of Bolton*

INTRODUCTION

In sitting down to write this book I am only too well aware of how satisfying and yet how serious a task it will be. The satisfying side to this book is the opportunity it gives me, as one who has been an ordained minister, and some would say 'priest', in that part of the Church called the Anglican tradition, to reveal that throughout the whole of that ministry, of some 60 years, I have been a very active Freemason. I became a Freemason at the invitation, first of an Archdeacon and second, of a Canon of the local Cathedral, of whose similar faith and conviction as Christians and brethren I had no reason to doubt. Belief and brotherhood was not only represented by them but by the five other clergymen whom I was to see present in Lodge on the day of my initiation.

Nor was that all. Three years later, as the new Rector of the Manchester parish to which I had also been directed, I was asked one morning, by my own medical doctor who was also the churchwarden, where I was going to join locally as a Freemason. Never having mentioned my Masonic membership to anyone there I was somewhat surprised that he knew, and yet delighted that a staunch churchman was not only a Brother but was clearly eager to help me find a suitable Lodge – it turned out to be his.

It is satisfying, after all these years on, to be able to affirm my conviction as to the total compatibility of the two professions. In what follows I shall seek to show how that compatibility is possible for one who believes, as I do, and as Nicodemus had to learn, that you have to be born again if you are truly to live 'in Christ'. The truth, however, I must repeat, lies in the living of our faith and not just in the repeating of what we think are the right words. What I have to acknowledge here is the privilege that I am being offered of being able to record the convictions of a lifetime that I share with many others.

Very serious this story certainly is because we will be dealing with matters that I and millions of others in the world believe to be absolutely essential to one's life here and beyond the grave or the crematorium and the funeral pyre. There cannot be, I believe, and let me affirm this at the very outset, any greater issue than the basis on which one's faith rests. For me that basis is, and has been uninterruptedly since my earliest childhood, that God our Father so loved this world that as Jesus Christ, God the Son shared our human life and through the awful experience of the Cross of Calvary, by resurrection from the tomb of death and the continuing presence of the Holy Spirit, he made salvation available to all who, through a baptism of personal faith, become grace-full members of his Church.

That may be too brief a declaration of all that I in fact believe but for the moment it will have to suffice as it covers all the necessary elements of the ancient Christian creeds. Those creeds I have recited repeatedly believing in what they declare, and seeking humbly, if sometimes falteringly and inadequately, to represent in my living, and not just by speaking, those truths that God wants us to share with others. That is one very serious and important aspect of this book. Personal conviction continues to be an inviolable right for each Freemason.

What has also to be affirmed at the outset of this book is this. That from the very start of what we have, in England, known as Accepted Freemasonry, that is, from the later years of the reign of Queen Elizabeth I, it was clearly the intention of its members to establish its precepts and practices on a Christian faith as I have described it. Evidence to support this view will be part of what this book seeks to offer. We will also examine why and how this initial basis was adapted to a changing and broader membership and circumstances without making it impossible for any with a lively Christian conviction to continue in its ranks.

The purpose of all that is written here is to explain, as understandably and considerately as I can, why it is possible to be a devout and believing Christian and also a Freemason. I could of course give brief examples of numerous men I have known, from ordinary members of a congregation to bishops, who have, like myself, seen no conflict in pursuing the two forms of living. I am equally aware that there are some men who, with no less honesty and deep feeling, are sure that our one God is not happy for them to continue in the Craft. There are now not a few books written by, or about, such ex-Masons. My concern is that only their side of the story seems so often to be told and that those of us who will have had a quite different experience are either not heard or ignored. Of course there may be some who read these pages who sincerely doubt whether I am telling the truth. I, certainly, have had the sad experience of being told by a fellow Anglican cleric that, since I was also a Freemason, he would not believe a word that I said on the subject. I would, he seemed convinced, be bound to misrepresent, or even conceal, the facts about this organisation which he was sure to be right about even though he had never actually belonged to it.

Since I have been a practising Christian and Freemason for so much of my life I do hope that whilst some readers may not agree with the conclusions I draw they will at least give some time to ponder on what are the facts that I lay before them and check them, if they wish, in the documents that I mention. Too many accusations regarding the so-called content of Freemasonry have been made which are grossly inaccurate. If they were true I would have left the Craft myself long ago. It is because I do know what is, and what is not, said and done in the whole of English Freemasonry's established ceremonies that I can claim to write on *Belief and Brotherhood* with the confidence that what is written can be relied on.

I am also well aware that what I shall have written by the close of this book will by no means be all that could be said on the many aspects of the faith and Freemasonry. The publishers were clear that this was not to be an exhaustive, and certainly not an exhausting, book on the subject. For those who want to pursue some areas further I would recommend that they read the much fuller treatment of Faith and Freemasonry that is contained in a book by a friend of mine, Kit Haffner, entitled *Workman Unashamed*, first published in 1985. Between us, I think it might be said, we will have provided for all tastes the authentic facts on which a proper assessment of the Craft by Christians can be made. Of course there may still be those who adopt the well-known view: "I know very well what the Masons are up to so don't confuse me with facts." To those who adopt such a stance I would respectfully refer the words of my Lord and theirs when he was faced with those who were so sure that he was wrong: "Why do you not understand what I say? It is because you cannot bear to hear my word." (The Gospel of John chapter 8, verse 43)

It is also my hope that what is written here will encourage others who have in the past felt the need to relinquish their Masonic membership, because of doubt about the compatibility between their faith membership and the Craft, to reconsider their decision and again belong to both. The Craft needs good men of faith, and the Church needs to have its men setting their own example and sharing their special influence in our Masonic society. Certainly I shall be delighted if what I have written answers serious doubts, creates informed debate and diminishes the misunderstanding that so easily feeds our prejudice. I pray that the tolerance that is such a feature of true Freemasonry might be extended through what is now to be shared. I, for one, have no regrets whatever that I was reared in sure Belief and introduced to a kindly Brotherhood.

It only remains in this introduction to draw attention to three matters that can assist the reader. The first thing is to stress that what follows applies almost wholly to Freemasonry in England and Wales. I really have no right to talk about the Craft in Scotland and Ireland and I must urge the reader to recognise that matters in the USA are distinctly different and in some instances involve unacceptable wording and practice. In particular the work of Bro. Pike, and not least his major work, *Morals and Dogma*, reflects in many parts a form of Masonry that is not ours.

The second matter is to note that the two books that will largely occupy us as works critical of Freemasonry are *Darkness Visible* by the Revd Walton Hannah, published first in 1950, and *Freemasonry – A Religion?* by the Revd John Lawrence, published in 1987.

The other matter is one of type usage and in particular of lower case and capital letters. For too long there has been misunderstanding and confusion about what kind of masons and Masonry we are talking about. In this, as in all my recent books I have chosen to use lower case initials for anyone or anything to do with operative masonry but to use capital initials for what refers to Accepted Masonry. A lodge on a work site can thus be easily distinguished from a ceremonial Lodge attached to a Guild. Similarly, a master mason engaged in the design and construction of a cathedral is very different to a Master Mason in present Freemasonry. Now we can also talk more sensibly about masons of the Middle Ages without our thinking these were the Masons of the modern Craft.

A LITTLE BIT OF HISTORY

If there is one aspect of previous critiques of Freemasonry from a religious standpoint which seems to be inadequate, it is the failure to take proper note of the Craft's history. I am aware, of course, that Walton Hannah wrote the following at the outset of his book, *Darkness Visible*:

"The scope of this work is not to give a history of Freemasonry in its development from the Catholic guilds or lodges of operative stone-masons in the Middle Ages through the speculative and Deistic seventeenth and eighteenth centuries to the pan-religious non-Christian universalism which the Craft upholds today." (op. cit. p. 9)

I might respectfully point out that that review seems like a condensed but quite extensive historical judgement indeed. It was, I am sure, certainly intended to set the scene for the very doubtful, if not unsavoury, doings that Masons are supposed to get up to when they gather for their Lodge meetings and hence no Christians should be involved. Fr. Hannah was, I regret, quite incorrect on a number of points, even in that short survey, as I shall shortly seek to show.

At least he went on to admit that it was possible to discover all the information he required about this so-called SECRET society. He further acknowledged that the rulers of Freemasonry in England "have imposed no effective check on the public sale of printed rituals (&) these manuals, rightly interpreted, do therefore give a reliable guide to Lodge workings. "However," he concludes, there is "only one Masonic secret that has been tolerably well-kept, especially from Masons. And this secret is the fact that there is no such thing as a specific Masonic secret." (op. cit. pp. 10, 11) We shall have to see later whether his final conclusion is also correct.

All this, in one sense, is a better view of present Freemasonry than that which so many members of the English public still have as to the mysterious, mystic, macabre and unfathomable origins of the Craft.

This view has, of course, been more than adequately fuelled by the emergence of such books as *The Brotherhood, The Holy Grail, The Hiram Key* and its successors, *The Da Vinci Code* and numerous lesser works. In particular the Templar theory has led us a merry, though wholly unrealistic, dance, especially through one old Scottish chapel. We must be grateful, however, that not long ago those who have wanted to have the true view of so-called Templar involvement can now read *The Rosslyn Hoax?*. As the author of that work, Robert Cooper, the Librarian to the Grand Lodge of Scotland, has written:

"All the essential elements of the modern myth were created during the Romantic period when a nostalgic view of the chivalric codes of the Middle Ages were fashionable and which culminated in not only physical displays of chivalry (e.g. the Eglinton Tournament) but also in a host of artistic and literary works. At a time when Scottish culture was fashionable and when there was a widespread belief that chivalry could still be relevant, a romantic Scottish Masonic chivalric Order was synthesised – the present K.T. The myth as we know it today was created by the Masonic KT of Scotland … Here lies the crux of the matter." (op. cit. p. 251)

The fact is that there is no secret, unknowable and unpalatable history that is yet to be uncovered, and at least in England the Grand Lodge has declared that Freemasons can now share openly with, and answer the uncertainties of, any enquirer. It is because of such a recent, refreshing change of attitude that a book like this, as well as others that I have written, could be published.

What is certain is that if the reader, especially if he or she is a non-Mason, (and yes, there are women who are Freemasons and proud of it) is not aware of the TRUE history of Masonry in this country then it is more than likely that they will not appreciate why Masons still do today what their forebears did and why. The constant feature of most criticisms of this Society is that it is treated as if it was suddenly thought up in the comparatively recent past and so contains features that ought never to have been introduced or countenanced by the faithful Church members of today. That is neither a correct nor a proper assessment of Freemasonry's link with its long traditions.

It is therefore necessary for me to present, at the outset of this book, an up-to-date but also fuller summary of just that overview of our history which Fr. Hannah sought to present above. This is not given here with any intention of scoring points but so that as I come to the detailed points of Masonic practice in what follows a reader will have a more correct backcloth against which the ceremonies still passed through by Masons can be fairly judged. So this is the story.

It is now clear that following the devastating effects of the Black Death in the middle of the 14th century regulations were introduced by the Crown to combat the new, excessive wage demands, employment of irregular workmen, unacceptable levels of quality in products and many other work problems. The trades in each city or town were required to renew, and if necessary revise, their charters and supply evidence of the antiquity and traditional rules of their craft. Admission to those guilds was for Freemen only, that is, men who were now free of the indentures which they had signed as apprentices for a normal seven-year period. On their entry to a masons' guild, which incidentally would be dedicated to the Blessed Virgin Mary and the two Saints John, the Baptist and the Evangelist, these Catholic men, and some women who were widows or sisters of Freemen, pledged themselves upon the Holy Gospels to abide by the regulations and customs, and especially the secrets of the mason trade, and sealed it with a penalty which was EXACTLY THE SAME as that used for a like purpose until quite recent times in our Masonry.

Much play is made of the ferocity and savagery of these oaths as John Lawrence illustrated in 1987: "Assuming that the initiate is willing, he must next undertake a 'solemn obligation', in other words, swear an oath on the Bible never to reveal in any way the secrets or mysteries of the craft to a non-mason. This is made under a threat of barbaric punishment: that of his throat being cut and his tongue torn out. These penalties still prevail in freemasonry in spite of some outcry against them. As a compromise, in 1964 permissible alternatives were sanctioned which speak of 'ever bearing in mind the traditional penalty ...', but which in fact still have the effect of causing the candidate to appreciate that these rituals contain something deeply secretive which must not in any circumstances be revealed to, or even discussed with those outside." (*Freemasonry – A Religion?* pp. 67ff)

In the 15th century of which we were originally speaking men and women were regularly being burnt at the stake if they refused to obey church requirements. On the other hand a mason was instructed in how, if, as a result of faulty workmanship, he rendered a block of expensive stone unusable, he was no longer put to death as had been the case in earlier times but the damaged stone was borne like a dead person on a funeral bier to be cast off among the rubbish, whilst he was severely reprimanded and heavily fined. The harsh penalty above, set in that context, as still remembered by us, was then a severe warning to ensure strict silence about the masons' work secrets.

What was considered necessary and acceptable for our forebears was for long retained as part of Guild tradition, because we still used their trade name. Nowadays that form is NO LONGER used at a candidate's making of his promise but it is still mentioned in the course of the ceremony so as to recall the history of previous practice. In Scotland and Ireland Masons have made no changes whatever, and they are still using the same words. Their adherence to tradition is clearly more hardy than ours.

That, of course, is far from being the end of the story. By the end of Edward VI's reign in 1553 not only had there been the destruction of the monasteries, their hospitals, and the chantry chapels but all the parish and saints guilds that were an integral part of medieval community life. In his 2003 work, *Reformation*, Prof. Diarmaid MacCulloch wrote this:

"... the great unifying theme of late medieval religion was prayer (and the) main institutions designed for this, both in the south and in death-absorbed northern Europe, were called gilds, brotherhoods, sisterhoods or confraternities: a variety of descriptions for the same basic institution. These were voluntary organisations, bound by oath and a membership levy, with common activities and purposes ... but virtually all had some concern with prayer for the membership. In northern Europe especially, a gild might create a chantry, with its own altars for gild Masses in a chapel building, possibly forming part of a parish church. An important aspect of these essential vehicles of late medieval religion was that they were run by the laity, who paid the gild clergy ..." (op. cit. p. 16) When such a widespread segment of parish life was dissolved and forbidden it can be imagined what an impact that had on popular devotion and religious practice. Fortunately the trade guilds were not closed down but even they, in the 1570s, suffered the loss of no longer being allowed to present the trade, or mystery, biblical plays.

However, what we now know is that in addition to keeping their guild COURT that administered the trade, the stonemasons, and they alone, had set up a permanent lodge attached to their guild to preserve their history and customs. What now happened was that, at least in York and London, but almost certainly elsewhere, Freemen who had no guild of their own or who were attracted to the lodge because of its reputation for antique history, legends and practices, began to apply for membership. This was timely for the masons who, because there had been a serious diminution in the call for stone building and repair, and a new craze for building in brick and timber, had seen a fall in the number of working stonemasons as Freemen. There was therefore a natural desire to welcome any possible new candidates as guild members. Since these new members were not authentic, operative masons they began to be known as Accepted Masons to signify their special relationship. Here are the beginnings of what has become modern Freemasonry in which our members are called 'Free and Accepted Masons'.

The newly accepted members began to bring into the Lodge topics and practices, which were being cultivated by the new Grammar Schools. These included a fuller acquaintance with Scripture, a freer use of prayer, the method of catechetical instruction as in the new parish forms of instruction and in psalm singing. They also introduced the rediscovered classical stories of Greek and Roman antiquity. That is why the basis of all Lodge instruction now became the expanded Old Charges that brought the history of Masonry up to their present time. It is only recently that it has been realised afresh how much more needs to be learnt from these sources, but to give some idea of how relevant they are to our present subject I quote from the Grand Lodge No. 1 Ms. of 1583. It starts with a solemn prayer: "The might of the Father of Heaven and the Wisdom of the Glorious Son through the grace and the goodness of the Holy Ghost, that be three persons and one God, be with us at our beginning; and give us grace so to govern us here in our living that we may come to His bliss that never shall have ending. Amen."

Is it now surprising if I point out that throughout the seventeenth century the ethos of a Masonic Lodge was recognisably Christian with Anglican, Presbyterian and Roman Catholic members happily taking part in their proceedings? Verifiable evidence of the form of words used in what we call 'ritual' in such meetings is not so far available until 1696 in the Edinburgh Register House Ms. unless we consider a form of Heredom working which was to reappear in the 1730s. In what was that first document we read: "You make him (a candidate), take up the bible and laying his right hand on it you are to conjure him to secrecie." After a short interval in which a new member is taught how to behave in the Lodge he re-enters and says, "As I am sworn by God and St. Jhon (sic)" thus indicating that the earlier Saints were still honoured in what was now to be know as 'Old St. John's Masonry'.

In another document called the Dumfries Ms. of 1710 we have the following catechism:

Q. how many steps was in jacob's ladder?
A. three

Q. what was they?
A. A father son and holy spirit

Q. how many flowers in ye mason's posey?
A. 3 and 12

Q. what call you them?
A. trinity & ye twelve Apostles …

Q. what was ye greatest wonder that (was) seen or heard about the temple?
A. god was man and man was god, mary was a mother and yet a maid …"

Not only is it wrong to brand seventeenth-century Masonry as Deist in spirit but this is now recognised as unjustified in the eighteenth century despite the well-known phrase in what we call the 1723 Constitutions about 'observing that religion in which all men agree'. What that would have meant at that time was that following the sad experience of the English Civil War and the current religious wars in Europe, Masonry was wanting to provide a meeting place where those of differing political as well as religious opinions could meet as fellow-citizens. This is the kind of forum, which a Lodge has continued to be. As far as religion was concerned the plan was to avoid the conflicts of denominationalism. Hence the agreed basis for belief in the Brotherhood was to be common biblical information and if there were an overall pattern it was at least Theist. Since it is often cause for complaint that God is referred to in initial Freemasonry as 'The Great Architect of the Universe' it was such a name for God that Dr. Stillingfleet, Archbishop of Canterbury, often employed in his 18th-century sermons.

It has to be realised, however, that from the 1730s there was a growing dissatisfaction in the Craft about what was regarded as the failure to re-instate many features of what was earlier mentioned, Old St. John's Masonry. One of the main items of this complaint was that the premier Grand Lodge was not retaining enough of the directly Christian references in the ritual. Indeed, members of the eventual Antients Grand Lodge – called Antient because they sought to recover old ways – used prayers that were addressed to Jesus Christ. What is notable in this case was that as an increasing number of Jewish men sought membership in their Lodges the Antients directed that for their introduction, though the Bible would be opened as usual at the passage in St. John's Gospel, chapter 1, these candidates would be allowed a Hebrew prayer of admission. This both retained the traditional Christian ethos of the Craft whilst allowing the toleration that was meant to distinguish this Brotherhood in the England of that day. It needs to be stressed that even today, when a member of another faith is to be admitted, the whole Bible has to be openly displayed even if the candidate's hands are laid on what he regards as his holy scripture. The Christian basis and context of an English Lodge is thus preserved.

Referring further to the rapid, but sadly misleading, brief summary by Fr. Hannah we need finally to consider his judgement of the decisions made in 1813. These were made to recast the future rituals of Freemasonry so as to permit all the members of the then expanding British Empire to share in the benefits of our Masonic Brotherhood. He called it "pan-religious non-Christian universalism" when he knew very well that our Freemasonry proscribes all religious, as well as political, debate and distinction in its gatherings and certainly has no religious programme to pursue. If I sit in a Lodge in Israel, as I was recently invited to do, where Jewish, Muslim and Christian members assemble for a lecture on our Craft, is that not something which, in the present climate in that land, we should as Christians be glad about? Incidentally, the Duke of Sussex, who as Grand Master encouraged and oversaw the change in the 1813 approach to ritual, was himself a declared Christian, a President of the British and Foreign Bible Society and a learned student of the original texts of that Holy Book. It was also in order to avoid the accusation of denominational bias that that Society held its first meetings in Freemasons' Hall, in London.

This little bit of history has almost run its course, but before it ends there is one more facet of this part of our story that needs to be mentioned. In the course of the nearly 450 years of what began to be the Freemasonry known today it is a remarkable fact that despite the still overall Christian background of this Society of men there have been continual admissions of those from other faiths who have somehow sensed that whatever might be the attitude to them in the day-to-day world outside they are welcomed here as the brethren of those whom they have now joined. That was certainly the experience of countless Jews in the 18th century who were admitted here on the square when they were, and in some places still are, excluded from some associations. For some Muslims this same experience is beginning to be true. In a society where they can experience avoidance or rejection here, one can believe, some of them will find acceptance and respect for them as men of faith. Is the Lodge then not a place where some Christians, and even some Christian clergy, ought to be? But even as I say that, I know that there are those who think that there are so many other drawbacks to membership as a Mason that even a legitimate history will not suffice. It is therefore to those other obstacles that I must now turn.

WHY IS THERE CONCERN?

I never had the slightest idea that anything, which Dan Brown would write in his latest novel, *The Lost Symbol*, would be of assistance in my present work. Yet this is what he offers us on pp. 30–32 of his book. Professor Langdon is addressing students in a lecture theatre and has just explained how the city of Washington was first laid out according to star plans, which were carefully followed, by architects and sponsors who were also Freemasons. On some part of all the principal buildings a sign of the Zodiac was carved because in early Middle Eastern culture the zodiac represented God's overall design as creator of the heavens. This provoked an animated response from his audience, as follows:

"My uncle is a Mason," a young woman piped up. "And my aunt hates it because he won't talk about it with her. She says Masonry is some kind of strange religion."

"A common misconception." (says the Professor)

"It's not a religion?"

"Give it the litmus test," Langdon said, "Who here has taken Professor Witherspoon's comparative religion course?"

Several hands went up.

"Good. So tell me what are the three prerequisites for an ideology to be considered a religion?"

"ABC," one woman offered. "Assure, Believe, Convert."

"Correct," Langdon said. "Religions assure salvation, religions believe in a precise theology, and religions convert non-believers." He paused. "Masonry, however, is batting zero for (all) three. Masons (when acting just as Masons) make no promises of salvation, they have no specific theology and they do not seek to convert you. In fact, within Masonic lodges, discussions of religion are prohibited."

"So … Masonry is anti-religious."

"On the contrary. One of the prerequisites for becoming a Mason is that you must believe in a higher power. The difference between Masonic spirituality and organised religion is that the Masons do not impose a specific definition or name on a higher power. Rather than definitive theological identities like God, Allah, Buddha or Jesus, the Masons use more general terms like Supreme Being or Great Architect of the Universe. This enables Masons of different faiths to gather together."

"Sounds a little far out," someone said.

"Or perhaps, refreshingly open-minded," Langdon offered. "In this age when different cultures are killing each other over whose definition of God is better, one could say the Masonic tradition of tolerance and open-mindedness is commendable." Langdon paced the stage. "Moreover, Masonry is open to men of all races, colours and creeds, and provides a spiritual Fraternity that does not discriminate in any way."

"Doesn't discriminate? … How many WOMEN are permitted to be Masons, Professor Langdon?" (op. cit. pp. 30, 31)

A little while later Prof. Langdon presents them with the following: "Don't tell anyone but on the pagan day of the sun god Ra, I kneel at the foot of an ancient instrument of torture and consume ritualistic symbols of blood and flesh."

The class looked horrified.

Langdon shrugged. "And if any of you care to join me, come to the Harvard chapel on Sunday, kneel beneath the crucifix, and take Holy Communion."

The classroom remained silent.

Langdon winked. "Open your minds, my friends. We all fear what we do not understand." (op. cit. p. 32)

Grateful as Freemasons must be for this contemporary and widely circulated explanation about what is the subject of my present book, that Masonry is NOT a rival religion nor is it meant to be a substitute for it, there are a few of the statements here, put in the mouth of Prof. Langdon, that require further comment, especially by English Masons.

Referring to the concern of the aunt who much disliked her husband's unwillingness to speak about the Craft with her, I have to say that my own experience of American Freemasonry is somewhat different. The Brethren there have always seemed to me to be ready to talk about Masonry in the presence of non-Masons and are certainly not averse to wearing rings, tie-pins and lapel badges which openly proclaim their membership. We in England and Wales have never developed a similar use of such ornaments lest we might be suspected of favouring our own members, trying to influence others, gaining profit from, or boasting of, our membership. We have now escaped from the restriction of not talking openly with members of our family, and there is much more involvement of wives or partners when anyone seeks admission to our Order. I have recently suggested in one of my books what a Brother can say to his family after his Initiation. Secrecy about being a Mason, its history or its meaning need no longer be the case here. Not only are wives, older sons and daughters invited with potential candidates to introductory talks about Freemasonry but these are often held in the very Lodge rooms in which our ceremonies are conducted. It is, of course, true that none of this openness was encouraged prior to the 1980s.

Why not women Masons?, asked one student. Well, whatever the situation may be in the USA, the fact is that for over a century women too have been made Freemasons in England and Wales. In their principal organisation they practise exactly the same ceremonies and rituals as those practised by many of the men. I say 'many' because there are a number of varied rituals used in English and Welsh Lodges whereas the women have elected to use the form known as Emulation. It is mainly in Scotland that the women have adopted the rite of the Eastern Star also mentioned by Dan Brown.

When Prof. Langdon was commenting on the use of definite identities for the Deity he was not correct in excluding the term "God" for at the very outset of an English Freemason's membership he is asked this question, 'In all cases of difficulty and danger in whom do you put your trust?' The reply that is required to permit further progress is 'In God'. That same term is repeated later, not least when in the Charge to the new Mason, before he takes his seat amongst us, he is directed to remember his duty to God, his neighbour and himself. It is true that other sacred names are not now used in the basic 4 degrees but I shall be explaining how the Christian names of the Trinity are still very much part of current English and Welsh practice elsewhere.

It is possible, I suppose, for some people to misinterpret a further remark of Prof. Langdon's when he points out that the avoidance of specific names for the Deity "enables Masons of different faiths to gather together". Ah, but what do they gather together to do?, a critic may ask. Isn't this the path to a syncretistic position in which a Christian Mason has to acknowledge the parity of all beliefs and so surrenders his conviction in the uniqueness of God at work in Jesus Christ by the power of the Holy Spirit?

The answer is most definitely NO, because, as I can vouch from a lifetime of participation, no topic of a dogmatic or theological nature is ever broached in meetings of a Lodge or Chapter. This does not mean that if, in the interval between a meeting and the following meal, or at the meal itself, I was to ask a Muslim brother why Ramadan was so important to him or a Jewish member why he rightly expects kosher food, that this is a problem. In these circumstances, or in the privacy of his or my own home, matters of information are not an issue. What it is important to stress is that when a man, or woman, comes into the precinct of a Lodge or Chapter they are protected from credal interference or dogmatic encroachment. This is most important because no possible candidate should fear that his personal faith will be either questioned or imperilled. By the same token none of us sees our personal faith invaded or affected. What we come into Lodge to do is deal with those matters that are traditional in the Craft, the ancient paths of virtue, science and care.

It was in the years after 1965, however, that a growing concern about the legitimacy of Masonic membership for devout Christians began to occupy the attention of English Churches. Though we shall come in another chapter to the fuller story of that development we are to consider here what was probably the seedbed of that outcrop. It was the publication of the book *Darkness Visible*, written by the Revd. Walton Hannah and mentioned earlier. The title of this work recalled some words used in Masonic ritual, that first appeared in the poem 'Paradise Lost' by the Presbyterian, John Milton, and were repeated in *The Dunciad* by the Roman Catholic, Alexander Pope. The book was a comprehensive and critical study of all things Masonic and whilst acknowledging "the personal sincerity of the individual Christian Freemason" Hannah yet sought to present many of the features accepted by Masons that ought to give a convinced Christian serious food for thought. Not to put too fine a point on it he obviously hoped that after the revelations that he made no committed Christian, and certainly no bishop or priest, should continue as a member of the Order.

John Lawrence clearly felt that the same outcome was to be desired. "My contention is," he wrote, "that it is simply not possible to stand alongside a non-Christian and utter a prayer which he finds acceptable because it obviates the need for Christ as mediator, without changing the whole basis of our faith. The cross has opened the kingdom of God to men whose faith and allegiance is given over to Christ." (op. cit. p. 126) He then goes on to quote the passage in 2 Corinthians that states: "Do not be bound together with unbelievers." (Chap 6 v. 14) In a very real sense these writers were concerned on numerous counts regarding the apparent requirements laid on a Freemason and so in what follows I shall seek to offer the reader the most reasonable answers I can to issues that these two writers have raised except those already dealt with and those touching the other degrees that I will deal with later.

Before I tackle these individual issues, however, it would, I think, be useful to clarify a quite major point of difference between an English and Welsh view of the degrees and that taken elsewhere. The stance adopted in our two countries is the one spelt out in 1813 when the two Grand Lodges of the Antients and Moderns were at last united. It was then declared that Antient Masonry consisted of three degrees, the Entered Apprentice, the Fellowcraft and the Master Mason, together with the Order of the Holy Royal Arch. This meant that for English and Welsh Masons the culmination of the essential Craft was by being exalted to, and attaining, the three Chairs of the Holy Royal Arch. In Scotland and Ireland the culmination is becoming a Master Mason and being eligible to occupy the chair of Master of a Lodge, whilst in the USA it is, as Dan Brown continually emphasises, the attainment of what is called the 33rd degree of the Ancient and Accepted Scottish Rite. As other commentators in England continue to make much of this latter attainment in Freemasonry they need to know that this Order had its origin in France, where it consisted of 18 degrees, came to this land from the USA where it was at first one of 25 degrees and only latterly of 33, and certainly does not rank with the other degrees mentioned above as far as true ancient English working is concerned. I shall, however, say more about the Rose Croix, which is how we refer to it, when we come to the chapter on the Christian orders (chapter 4).

Let us now turn, however, to the half-dozen issues that seem to be of most concern to critics of the Craft from a religious point of view. And though the first of these has already been touched on it is of such crucial importance that I must address it again. This is the matter of a Mason's personal faith being jeopardised by more modern ritual forms in which the name of Jesus Christ is not mentioned.

Before I come to the core of my response to this very real anxiety

I must ask the reader to recall that the fount from which present Freemasonry springs is, and always was intended to be, Christian. A form of ritual which has been in use from the 17th century to the present day uses the closing words as follows:

"Tis finished. The Redeemer cried,
And lowly bowed His gracious head;
And soon the fainting sacrifice
Sunk down to regions of the dead.
Tis done! 'tis done! The noble work is done,
For men and angels far too great,
Which none but God's Eternal Son
Durst attempt or could complete."

It is not only because all original ritual was of this tradition but also because to this day no English or Welsh Lodge can function unless the whole Bible, from Genesis to the Book of Revelation, is open, displayed and referred to. Every new candidate for Freemasonry is addressed with these words before he takes his seat in a Masons' Lodge:

"Let me recommend to your most serious CONTEMPLATION the Volume of the Sacred Law, charging you to consider it as the UNERRING STANDARD of TRUTH and justice, and to regulate your actions by the DIVINE PRECEPTS it contains; therein you will be taught the important duties you owe to God … by never mentioning His name but with that AWE and REVERENCE which are due from the creature to his Creator, by imploring his AID in ALL your undertakings, and by looking up to Him in every emergency for comfort and support."

This is the most natural conclusion of a ceremony which began with the query, 'In all cases of danger and difficulty in whom do you put your trust,' and the answer required is 'In God.' Contrary to what many who have criticised the faith of Freemasons have claimed, there are two things needed that should be specially noted. The first is that this query is addressed to the individual concerned. It requires of each individual a personal response. What this means is that every Mason is expected to have his own private appreciation of a divine power in whom he puts his trust. A new member is not being asked to subscribe to some belief pattern peculiar to the Mason Craft, what some misguidedly call 'a Masonic God'. His declaration of faith is his own personal business which, in this Society that he now joins, will never be discussed or questioned and will certainly never be compared, favourably or otherwise, with that of any other Mason. What that then means, and it is important that we also spell this out at this point, is that as far as the Freemasonry of today is concerned there is not, nor for the last two centuries has there been, any separate concept of the Deity which a Brother (male or female) has been required to acknowledge. The only concept of God which a Freemason acknowledges is that with which a new member comes into Masonry and it is that concept, and that concept alone, that embraces every spiritual act that may occur in the various ceremonies that follow. When a Freemason prays, sings hymns, makes promises or engages in devout duties it is ALL done, in the name and in the presence of, that very God whom the individual personally reveres.

What that means in this author's case is, and for my lifetime has been, that the whole of what I am doing in this Masonic community is done in the name of the Holy Trinity, of God as Father, Son and Holy Spirit. If the Mason alongside me is acting faithfully in the name of his own deity that is his private business and right. He does not expect me to accept what he believes about God and, in this setting, I do not ask him to accept my understanding and belief. At this stage and in this circumstance we agree to have our own private view of who the God is in whom we place our trust.

I said earlier that when a new Mason is asked in whom he puts his trust there were two issues that were often overlooked. The second of these is this. The new member is taken on trust as knowing which God it is that he or she is acknowledging. It is not for nothing that our first intimations of a new kind of Accepted Freemasonry begin to emerge in the reign of Queen Elizabeth I because prior to her reign it was highly likely that the craftsmen who formed the guild of stonemasons would all have been Catholics according to the old religion; but now, after the brief resurgence of Queen Mary's rule, the religious opinions of the guildsmen would have begun to vary and what mattered most was their skill as craftsmen and not their personal religious opinions. As non-craftsmen joined the Guild Lodge this would become even more the case. It is worth remembering that it was Queen Elizabeth who declared that she was not concerned to pry into her people's hearts as long as they conformed to parish worship (See P. Collinson, *Elizabethan Essays* pp. 87ff). It is hardly surprising therefore that in Masonry as it then developed there was retained this practice of not examining what each member personally believed as long as he showed that he was "not a stupid atheist nor an irreligious libertine". It was precisely that trust between the members that enabled both this Society and that which was called the 'Royal Society' to function and grow.

There will be those, no doubt, who may regard this way of behaving as unacceptable because it seems to forfeit such opportunities for sharing one's faith with others or tacitly approving their understandings of God as comparable to one's own. If that represents what in fact takes place in a Lodge then such criticism would be both relevant and fair. That then gives rise at once to the proper question, "What is it that you Masons get up to when you meet?"

As Fr. Hannah has himself already admitted, there are now no impediments to discovering all that takes place in a Lodge. It is, of course, not just a case of knowing what happens and what is said but of understanding correctly the significance of those events. Let us begin with the matter of being first admitted as a candidate.

Fr. Hannah speaks of "the rather ludicrous humiliation of the preparation for initiation". That a bishop should, "in the name of the Great Architect, be deprived of his Episcopal ring and pectoral cross along with other articles of metal, and be blindfolded, haltered and partially undressed in search of Masonic light of which the Church in her fullness of grace knows nothing … superficially seems lacking in dignity and propriety," and even for a priest. (op. cit. p. 43)

The key word in this obviously concerned outburst is SUPERFICIALLY. If what he describes, as regards a bishop, were true then it does seem very undignified indeed. Let me at once affirm that that is something that I cannot imagine happening because if a clergyman has not become a Mason before he is elevated to the episcopate then it is very unlikely that this will happen later, not just because, as I now understand it, there is a general move not to consider for ordination anyone who is connected with the Craft, but also because a Bishop is likely to be so occupied with his new duties that entry into any new, regular commitment of time is extremely unlikely. If there are still bishops who are Freemasons it is because they entered our Brotherhood as clergy or even before ordination.

Fr. Hannah, of course, extends the sense of indignity, in the form of initiation, to a parish priest or even, as in my own case, to a humble curate. Some help is therefore required to explain why just looking SUPERFICIALLY at this procedure is not as debasing or demeaning as it might at first appear. Certainly Fr. Hannah sought to make his point forcefully by publishing the picture of a candidate prepared for entry. (op. cit. opposite p. 32)

What an enquirer, and certainly a Freemason, ought to know is that what a candidate is meant to represent is a working craftsman of the Middle Ages. The craftsman came in an open-necked shirt, with knee-length breeches and a cord around his waist to secure them. Indeed, when a candidate comes to the next two degrees he still appears as such a craftsman. In the third degree he is presented in exactly the guise that I describe above. Yet why does he have first one leg and then the other uncovered? The answer lies in the development of our Craft. Originally, only Fellows were initiated into a lodge and they therefore came with open shirt, a cord and knee-length pants. By the year 1813 there were three degrees and new forms of ceremony, called 'Sussex' working after the Duke of that name. It was then the custom to distinguish Apprentices and Fellowcrafts by turning up alternate trouser legs and then having both rolled up when they became Master Masons. Whether that was a good idea when hitherto they had always been admitted in what is now the Master Mason form is a fair question but unless you understand that this is not meant to be a joke or an act of humiliation, but preparing a man to be the proper descendant in dress of his master craftsmen forebears, then it may be good for a laugh by the unknowing public. The sad truth is that most Freemasons are still equally unknowing about the origin of this introductory dress. It is time they were always told, even before they enter the Lodge for the first time. Ignorance only supplies fuel for ridicule.

It is also time to be clear about why the candidate has, as that above picture revealed, his eyes covered with a blindfold, and one foot covered with a slipper, which Masons have always described as 'slipshod'. That is where that word comes from, though now meaning 'incorrectly attired'. What do these two further apparent indignities represent?

The blindfold is NOT worn, as I was first taught, to prevent the candidate seeing the form of a lodge room or even the people then present because it is most likely these days that he will have been in such a room beforehand and have met many of the Lodge members at social events. The purpose of the blindfold is to teach 'trust'. For after the candidate has declared his trust in God the Master of the Lodge says to him, 'Right glad am I to find your faith so well founded; relying on such sure support you may … follow your leader with a firm but humble confidence, for where the name of God is invoked, we trust no danger can ensure.' The candidate now has, for a while longer, to rely on one of those whom he is to join but whom he cannot identify. It has nothing to do with secrets but is the next lesson in brotherly care.

The lesson which is meant to be conveyed by the wearing of a sandal or slipper is equally relevant to our theme since it refers to the passage in the Book of Ruth in the Bible, ch. 4, verses 1–10. Boaz, a man of some local eminence, comes to the gate of Bethlehem to oversee the transfer of a parcel of land belonging to a woman called Naomi who has come home from Moab. He tells the person who has the first right to the land that if he cannot purchase it he, Boaz, will do so, taking the widow, Naomi, and her daughter-in-law, Ruth, along with it. Boaz is in fact allowed to be the purchaser and then we read:

"Now in earlier times in Israel, for the redemption and transfer of property to become final, a party took off his sandal and gave it to the other. This was the method of legalising transactions in Israel." (v.7)

Boaz then removes his sandal and gives it to the kinsman to seal the transaction, saying: "Today you are witnesses that … I have also acquired Ruth the Moabitess, as my wife." It is this piece of ancient Jewish practice that is now being enacted by the wearing of the slipper or sandal. The slipper belongs to the Lodge that the candidate is to join and by accepting it the candidate becomes part of the family that owned the footwear. This is why in 18th-century ritual there is mention of a candidate 'having something of his mother's', referring to the sandal handed to him by his mother Lodge. So intimately is another part of the Bible story linked with our Craft, that being a part which involves Boaz and Ruth, the ancestors of King David and of Jesus Christ.

As we have now found ourselves immersed in the symbolism of a Mason's initiation we ought to complete the explanation by mentioning the cable-tow that is placed on the body, and the removal of all metallic objects, including money, before a man enters the Lodge room. In regard to the cable tow the same consideration has to be given to this as to the disclosure of different legs in the first two degrees. The cable tow finishes up around the waist of a Master Mason, which is where it was meant to be all along, both as a support for one's breeches and also as a protection in the true Master Mason's degree.

What is important to note is that this is a cable tow and not a halter suggesting slavery, as Fr. Hannah describes it, nor is it a rope or cord. It is a remnant of that original Noah Freemasonry which commemorated the saving of mankind from the flood by God, through the obedience of his servant Noah. We even have another momentary reference to the Christian basis of our Order because Noah was for medieval teachers a prototype of Christ, who also redeemed mankind. Anyone who wants to take this idea further should consider the maritime nature of the penalties mentioned with the obligations. Thus, when, and if, you want to know more, even the apparently secular punishments once repeated by our forefathers all had a relationship to original Christian teaching.

The removal of valuables and metallic objects was to remind candidates of whatever rank that it was not possible, either to buy your entry into the privileges of a craft, or to force your way into them. It is not how much you earn or what influence in society you may wield that secures you a place as a Mason. What matters is that you have a personal faith and a willingness to follow that life of virtue that your faith requires. But here we come to one of the major sticking points in the understanding of 'Belief and Brotherhood'.

The Revd John Lawrence stresses this matter in several ways. "I have spoken to a number of men who have told me that the craft satisfies needs that the church fails to meet – for example, the need for ceremonial, traditional presentation and a sense of mystery. ... This heightened god-consciousness is undoubtedly a form of 'cheap grace'. It is the granting of God's blessing and assurance in a false, man-made, man-centred way. Its religious basis appeals to an instinctive feeling that we are good enough to save ourselves. ... As we have seen earlier, the craft enforces the erroneous world-view that man has the power to attain the heavenly realm without recourse to a mediator. It is enough if he is good enough in his own eyes." (op. cit. pp. 130, 131, 133)

Fr. Walton Hannah is equally forthright. "On reading the ritual carefully Masonry … teaches one's whole duty to God and to man, and a way of justification by works which if followed will lead to salvation. Nowhere does it give the slightest hint that anything further is necessary to the religious life. It urges, it is true, the reading of the Volume of the Sacred Law, but as this may or may not be the Bible, the inference is obviously that moral precept rather than the doctrines of any particular Church or religion should be the object." (op. cit. p. 40)

Now these are quite serious charges, and certainly for any Christian priest or minister. They go to the very heart of what I certainly believe to be essential Christian belief and if the accusations were true then I must have spent the greatest part of my adult life sharing in what is directly contrary to what I have preached and taught in the majority of my life. So we must examine in some detail whether these claims are correct. I shall, for the most part, keep myself to the texts of what I outlined earlier as 'ancient Masonry', the three Craft degrees and the Holy Royal Arch. Though both the above writers also stray into other branches of Freemasonry I shall avoid doing the same because it is in the next two chapters that I shall also be dealing with further issues raised by them and others about the additional degrees.

I begin by looking at the content of the prayers used in the opening and closing ceremonies. In the Apprentice or first degree the Worshipful Master (W.M.) says, 'before I declare it open let us invoke the ASSISTANCE of the Great Architect of the Universe (G.A.O.T.U.) in ALL our undertakings …" and in closing, 'let us with all reverence and humility express our gratitude to the G.A.O.T.U. for favours already RECEIVED; may He continue to PRESERVE the Order by cementing and adorning it with every moral and social virtue.' (op. cit. pp. 86, 94) Why, if all our moral striving is our own unaided work do we here ask for God's assistance and thank him for the help that He has already given and for the further 'cementing and adorning' that we need?

In the second degree we 'supplicate the Grand Geometrician of the

Universe' that the rays of heaven may shed their influence, to enlighten us in the paths of virtue and science' at the opening, and, in closing, the W.M. reminds us that wherever we are and whatever we do, God is with us, 'and His all-seeing eye observes us, so let us discharge our DUTY to HIM with fervency and zeal.' (pp. 88, 92) Here again we look again to that God whom each Mason privately and personally reveres for HIS enlightenment in virtuous and wise pursuits, and remember that it is to him who is our daily companion that we are to direct our attention. Whilst in the third degree we specifically look to the One in heaven to AID our endeavours at the start and express 'All gratitude to the Most High' at the close. (pp. 89, 91) Why, again I ask, are we so continually voicing our need of, or appreciation for, divine direction or aid if we have no place for a mediator or implementer?

When we turn to the prayers that precede each of the subsequent ceremonies I find the same constant dependence on God in the conduct of our affairs. The reader must judge:

'Vouchsafe Thine AID, Almighty Father … and grant that this candidate for Freemasonry may so dedicate and devote his LIFE to THY service as to become a pure and FAITHFUL Brother among us. ENDUE him with a competency of Thy DIVINE WISDOM, that, assisted by the secrets of our Masonic art, he may the better be enabled to unfold the beauties of true GODLINESS, to the honour and glory of Thy Holy Name.' (p. 96) What is it that we are being told here? It is that aided and endued by God, and a God who is addressed as only Christians address the Deity, as Father, that a Mason is to serve his God to the honour of His Holy Name. It is true that we ask to be 'assisted' by what he can learn in our company, but it is with divine wisdom that we shall even more surely (not 'better' in superior sense) unfold 'true GODLINESS', not mere human achievement.

And what do we find in the prayer of the second degree? 'We supplicate the CONTINUANCE of thine aid, O merciful Lord, … may the work BEGUN in Thy Name, be continued to Thy GLORY, and evermore established in us by OBEDIENCE to Thy precepts.' From start to finish the whole of our endeavours are to be in the domain, and under the direction of, our Lord God. And lest any critic may want to suggest that 'O merciful Lord' must be an influence of Islam may I direct their attention to Jonah the prophet who learnt from his God that "thou art a merciful God". (ch.4. v. 2). In Luke ch. 6 v. 36 the "Father is merciful".

When we come to the third degree prayer we are almost overwhelmed by the emphasis on Divine initiative, for we read: "Almighty and Eternal God … at whose creative fiat all things first were made, we, the FRAIL creatures of Thy providence, humbly implore Thee to pour down … the continual dew of Thy blessing. Especially, we beseech Thee, to IMPART THY GRACE to this Thy servant …" (p. 132) Here, in the context of biblical truth, we, as God's created beings, need and ask for blessing and grace that we may pursue what is to follow. We shall look at what follows in the next chapter but at last we literally administer the 'coup de grace', for whenever a Provincial or Grand Chaplain offers prayer on special occasions he utters words that demolish utterly the very suggestion of any justification by works amongst Freemasons. He says,

"Almighty and Eternal God, WITHOUT whose special and prevenient GRACE ALL HUMAN WORKS are of no AVAIL …" Here is the answer to complete all the evidence that has gone before. For Freemasons, be they Christians or not, the seal is here set on the primacy and majesty of God in all human affairs. We need God at every stage of our human journey and Freemasons humbly acknowledge and receive that aid in all their undertakings. If it were not so, I repeat, my sojourn in the Craft would have ended long ago.

THE CRAFT DEGREES AND THE HOLY ROYAL ARCH

Several points in the rituals of these degrees about which non-Masons feel concern have already been mentioned and explained but it is still the case that there are sections that require our attention. Fr. Walton Hannah was so eager to make plain the grounds for his anxiety about a Christian's involvement in Freemasonry that he devoted half of his book, *Darkness Visible*, to reproducing in detail the rituals, and notes on them, that relate to the subjects of this chapter. If we are to treat his concerns seriously then we need to range more widely than we have done so far.

In the book by John Lawrence the Craft Degrees receive separate attention and a number of points clearly emerge. I have already sought to deal with the issues as to which God a Freemason is honouring and serving, and whether, as he contends, Freemasonry encourages justification by works and not Faith. It is essential to keep those explanations in mind because they are the basis on which much that follows depends.

This same author first takes up the candidate's invitation to undertake a solemn oath or promise to abide by the rules of the Society he is about to join. The statement by the W.M., that Masonry 'is founded on the purest principles of piety and virtue' and that the vows to be taken contain 'nothing incompatible with your civil, moral or religious duties' are, Lawrence claims, self-contradictory because Jesus alone is the truth as claimed in John's Gospel ch. 14 v. 6. At the risk of repeating myself unduly may I point out that the words heard by each candidate are based exactly on the very same vows, but WITH the original penalties, that were taken by our Catholic forebears in the stonemasons' guild. For them they were indeed based on the purest principles of their religion and were thus compatible with their religious duties.

That is the reason why I can accept them as a Christian today, but we must not forget that there are members of other faiths in the

Brotherhood who have to ask themselves how such words sound to them. I cannot answer for them nor they for me. For me the Christ of the Bible that is ALWAYS OPEN before me in the Lodge, is present, as in every part of my life, and what the W.M. asserts is therefore true for me. Of course I also believe, as Lawrence insists, that "For someone born again of the Spirit of God … there can be no place for any thing or anyone claiming equal or higher revelation" (p. 67) At no point in this vow, however, is anything like that suggested UNLESS a hearer assumes that 'our secret arts and hidden mysteries' must be of that nature. They were certainly not regarded in that way by the craftsmen who first took this obligation because these clearly meant trade secrets and methods, on which their very livelihood depended. Since those days these practical matters have changed into the moral lessons and guides that are in agreement with the teachings of that Bible which we are instructed to consult. It may be more alluring for John Lawrence to suppose "that these rituals contain something deeply secretive which must not in any circumstances be revealed" (p.68) but since, as Fr. Hannah admits, one can now have access to all our workings, where is the evidence for there being something more?

The perpetual conundrums, however, that seem to pervade all that this critic writes are these: what is it that he is asking of a Christian like myself? Does he want Freemasonry to be restored to its overtly Christian origin or does he want its evidently ancient tradition to be forsaken and left to others? But which others, and why? Further, does he recognise that Masonry is not a religion yet he seems to want it to be a false one? One really gets the impression that a Freemason cannot be right whatever he or she does or says. Creating such an attitude cannot be right by someone who claims that HE is a "born again Christian". What kind of a response is that to the words of Jesus, "let your yes be yes and your no, no"? (Matthew ch. 5 v. 37).

I did in the last chapter quote the words about the necessity of being guided by the contents of the Bible, which is clearly pointed out to a candidate. The W.M. here tells the candidate, who at once sees the Bible before him when he has his blindfold removed, that these 'Sacred writings GOVERN our faith' which should surely be a clear enough indication of the implied spiritual influence in this Society. It is very pertinent to remark here that Prof. Diarmaid MacCulloch has just written a history of Christianity covering 3000 YEARS because it is, he says, a fact that this faith begins in the Jewish writings and leads to a Jewish Messiah. The very presence of the complete Bible speaks volumes and its retention as an official landmark of Masonry is highly significant.

However, because it is true that at a new member's initiation he is permitted to take his obligation holding or touching his own sacred text, if not the Bible, Lawrence then claims that "Masonry holds that all volumes sacred to men (and presumably women) are equally valid." (p. 70) The truth is that in our Masonry no such statement has ever been made and when the 'Volume of the Sacred Law' (V.S.L.) is mentioned in Masonic texts it is the whole Bible to which it alone refers. John Lawrence is jumping to his own unfounded conclusions when he goes on: "It is intrinsic to Masonic belief that a higher revelation of God can be found, beyond that revealed by such sacred volumes … The Old Testament, as we shall see, is regarded as legend. Its stories are quarried to provide images and allegories that further Masonic teaching." (op. cit. p. 70) The matter of whether there is "a higher revelation of God" is clearly something to which we shall have to return but the assertion that the Old Testament is "legend" does not accord with the next two actions in which the candidate is involved.

He is told that the 'word' of this degree is BOAZ, which was the name in the Bible for the left-hand pillar of the porchway of the inner sanctum of King Solomon's Temple. It was the actual name of a real person, not legend, whom we have already met. There were also two pillars which did exist and which we will encounter further in the next degree.

We are then told that the W.M. invests the new member "with the distinguishing badge of a mason, an apron made of lambskin". This is not actually the case because, following ancient practice where the presiding officer in a lodge on a working site was the Warden, it is now he, the Senior Warden, who presents and attaches the apron. That it referred to Jesus as the Lamb of God (John ch. 1 v. 29) is true but it referred also to the Passover Lamb whose blood was placed on the doors of the Jews in Egypt to signify the innocence of those within and that is why the angel of death 'passed over' that house. (Exodus ch. 12 v. 13). It is to that real, not legendary, event that the Warden now refers when he says, 'It is the badge of innocence and the bond of friendship' – this bond being the sharing of the lamb at table, not least at the Last Supper of the twelve disciples with Christ. John Lawrence says that the Master's claim is "preposterous" because it suggests that by putting on the apron men reckon themselves innocent before God. They do not. It is all God's gracious act of atonement represented by what the Lamb signifies. To any Christian Freemason who is properly taught in the Scriptures there is no need for this to be spelt out whilst for the Brethren of any other faith they will have their own interpretation.

We are now introduced to the meaning of what were the three working tools of an original working apprentice mason. As we are no longer operative craftsmen these tools are given a moral application. John Lawrence here comments: "Throughout Masonic ritual there is constant reference to God and duty to him. The way of life under God encouraged by masons is very good and laudable. There is no doubt of that. It is in many ways 'the right way to live'." (p. 74) As he quotes the words used of the Gavel that "should keep down all vain and unbecoming thoughts," so that they might rise unpolluted and acceptable to God, he cannot resist the inference that this shows how men seek God's favour by such good behaviour. "Neither freemasonry nor any other life system, can make our thoughts and our actions 'unpolluted' and pleasing to God" (p. 75) But the words of our ritual state clearly that such 'words and actions may ascend unpolluted … to the Throne of Grace" which is where the Christian conscience derives its discernment in the first place, as was stated in the last chapter.

Moreover this writer fails to mention altogether the Apprentice Gauge which represents the 24 hours of the day, "part to be spent in prayer to Almighty God," which precedes our labour and refreshment, or our helping a friend or Brother in time of need. It is thus, as the Charge that is next to be delivered will underline, that we are to look up to God "in every emergency for comfort and support". Those of us who are Christians have not the slightest doubt where our true source of living lies. Why does not John Lawrence tell us that in the same Charge that completes a Freemason's admission he hears this: "enabling you to exert those talents WHEREWITH GOD HAS BLESSED YOU, as well to HIS GLORY, as the welfare of your fellow creatures" and closing with these words 'indelibly imprint on your heart the SACRED DICTATES (i.e. God's directives) of Truth, of Honour and of Virtue'? Even the explanation of the First Degree Tracing Board, which is still too rarely done, uses the words "The Universe is the Temple of the Deity WHOM WE SERVE …" and displays at its heart a ladder 'in Scripture called Jacob's ladder … It reaches to the Heavens, and rests on the Volume of the Sacred Law, because by the doctrines contained in that Holy Book, we are taught to believe in the dispensations of Divine Providence, which belief strengthens our faith, and enables us to ascend the first step …' Clearly, the proper progress of a Freemason depends on faith in the God revealed in the Bible.

At the end of this explanation there is reference to what was an ancient symbol of Freemasonry that appears on the face of the pedestal from which the ladder mentioned above rises. It was a circle flanked by two uprights | O |. At the beginning of what was to become modern Freemasonry, and when the catechetical teaching was overtly Christian, the parallel lines represented John the Baptist and John the

Evangelist, but when changes were made in the early 19th century these two uprights were named as Moses and Solomon. I think it can be seen that immediately the sign was more acceptable to both Jewish and Muslim believers whilst Christians also could accept these figures as God's chosen servants in Holy Scripture. The words attending this sign are of particular significance: 'and were we as conversant in that Holy Book, and as adherent to the doctrines therein contained as those parallels were, it would bring us to Him who would not deceive us, neither will He SUFFER DECEPTION.'

We pass now to the Second or Fellowcraft Degree, which John Lawrence reports as being considered by many Masons as something of an anti-climax. This is because, of course, this was originally the substantive degree and the admission of an Apprentice was a very simple appendage that preceded the step of becoming a Fellow. Following the formation of the premier Grand Lodge in London and Westminster the idea of three degrees, BEFORE occupying the Chair of a Lodge, was slowly developed and the old and unique Fellow degree was divided into the Apprentice and parts of a new Master Mason degree. When you know this you can better appreciate why, in this degree as it now stands, one has both a sense of repeating what was done in the previous degree but with an eventual sense of something more to follow. This is especially so when the meanings of the two pillar words are given together so that we have words said to have been uttered by God, 'In strength I will establish this mine house to stand firm for ever'. John Lawrence affirms that these are unscriptural words put into God's mouth but that is not altogether the case. As I mentioned in my book on the Craft, Mark and Chapter rituals the translation of the conjoint words is represented in 1 Kings ch. 8 v. 13: "Solomon said: I have built a mighty temple for you, a house for you to dwell in for ever".

John Lawrence also questions the use of the degree sign that is here communicated to the candidate as being derived purely from a legendary incident, not in the Book of Joshua. Our ritual says that this sign is based on it being 'in this position (that Joshua) prayed fervently to the Almighty to continue the light of day that he might complete the overthrow of his enemies'. This refers to the event in Joshua ch. 10 vv. 12, 13 where we read that: "On the day the Lord gave victory over the Amorites to Israel Joshua said to the Lord in the presence of Israel, 'O sun, stand still over Gibeon … so the sun stood still and the moon stopped, till the nation avenged itself over its enemies, as it is written in the book of Jashar.'

There is also another incident in the Book of Exodus ch. 17 vv. 10–13 that explains the position of the arms in praying at this time. While Joshua fought in a battle Moses raised his arms toward the sky and if his arms were weary Hur and Aaron supported them until Joshua won the battle. The care taken to provide a Scriptural basis for what was done should not be overlooked.

Also in connection with this degree there are those who question where the idea of a winding staircase with steps to the inner temple comes from. This was based on the joining of two actual features connected with Solomon's Temple. There were several separate courts for different groups on the way to the inner temple. One of these was the court of the women and to pass out of that there was a flight of steps leading to the court of the Israelitish men. Traditionally it was said to be made up of 15 steps. The other half of our 2nd degree feature was an internal, winding staircase, which began in the chamber reached through the southern wall of the Holy Place. It is best seen on the 1849 tracing board by Harris. What we learn from this feature's composition is the need to learn a great deal more about the Temple that still means so much to our Jewish brethren. It meant so much to Jesus, provided it was treated reverently.

At the end of his comments on this degree John Lawrence reproduces a statement by an early 20th century Masonic commentator, J.S.M. Ward, as follows: "This is the great lesson of the 2nd degree, that by ourselves and in ourselves, we can discover and realise God." John

Lawrence concludes: 'This is the lie that masonic ritual instils'. Insofar as Ward suggests that human beings BY THEMSELVES can discover God, and behave in such a way as to commend themselves to Him I would have to rebuff any such notion and refer to the ritual as proof. Thus, when asked how he 'hopes to obtain the privileges of the 2nd degree' the candidate answers, 'By the help of God' and he almost at once joins in prayer with us all 'while the blessing of Heaven is invoked on all we do'. In the prayer itself are the words: 'We supplicate the continuance of thine aid, O merciful Lord … may the work, begun in Thy name, be continued to Thy glory, and evermore be established in us by OBEDIENCE to THY PRECEPTS.' No, Bro. Ward is wrong and present readers can make up their own minds.

What is surprising about the rest of John Lawrence's comment at this point is that he does not pick up on the idea of any supposed justification by works but on another matter. Masonic ritual, he says, "interweaves biblical fact with masonic fiction, often derived from the mythology of ancient Egypt, Rome and India, making them all on a par". He is no doubt referring here to Ward's other books which make much use of such ancient writings but the reader should know that this line of study is now out of date and in no way representative of today's reliable studies. I have to add here that such books as *The Hiram Key* and its successors unhelpfully pursue this same path of historical inaccuracy. John Lawrence, however, pursues this theme to take us into the 3rd degree as follows: "As we look at the so-called Hiram Abiff we will see how this process takes on monumental proportions."

It is as we approach this degree, and the Holy Royal Arch that follows it, and with which it has always been tied, that we recognise our attitude of mind to be crucial. If our critics are determined to find something untoward and apparently in conflict with overt Christian teaching then their aim will probably be realised. If, however, as in my own case, I come as a life-long, devout Christian believer seeking how I may RIGHTLY concur with what I do and say in a Lodge at this point, then the result will be different.

From my standpoint I share in a prayer to a God whom I recognise as 'Almighty and Eternal, Architect and Ruler of the Universe,' who created all things and whose blessing we seek. We ask, as was also true in my own case, that the candidate amongst us will receive God's GRACE as he shares in what is to follow. It is only with such divine assistance that he can 'pass safely through the valley of the shadow of death (and) rise from the tomb of transgression'. Even when we come to the traditional 'Five points of Fellowship' that working masons had devised it includes a reminder of "my daily supplications that will properly direct me as to how I can assist others".

Furthermore, as we come to the summary by the W.M. of how we have come to this point in our Masonic progress we hear this: 'Above all, your admission among Masons in a state of helpless indigence, taught you to bend with humility and resignation to the will of the Great Architect of the Universe to dedicate your heart, THUS (i.e. by this means of submission to God) purified from every baneful and malignant passion, fit only for the reception of truth and wisdom, to HIS GLORY ...'

This commentary goes on to relate how we were led to use our minds even to recognising the very presence of God's Throne and it is in that awareness that the 'secrets of Nature and intellectual truth' are unveiled. It is NOW that we can face the moment of death, however tragic.

For those who find Freemasonry wanting from a Christian point of view their reading of these words is quite contrary. John Lawrence says (p.89): "I have quoted the first part of this exhortation at length since it is important that we get the context AND DETAIL and understand what craft freemasonry sees itself as being able to do. The clear assumption is that through masonry a man can stand before God, in some way purified, and enabled to receive truth and wisdom, to his glory." Yet he has not come to terms with the actual text for there is not the least acknowledgement that this is, "ABOVE ALL," dependent upon a bending to the WILL of God and the dedication of one's heart to God's glory. For him to conclude from this summary that "if this is to be believed then the very centre of Christianity is rendered obsolete" is quite unjustified. And such a biased interpretation carries on into what he thinks is the core of this degree.

"The object of worship in this degree," he writes, "is the unshaken fidelity and death of our Master Hiram Abiff." Respect for what is meant to be an example of 'unshaken fidelity and noble death' is what is here suggested but nowhere is there any hint of worshipping this figure. In the context of the Jewish Temple such a suggestion would be the utmost blasphemy especially to Jewish Masons.

Lawrence further writes, "No character in Scripture is called Hiram Abiff. There is a character 'called Hiram who was involved in the construction of the temple (see 1 Kings 7) and THIS IS THE ONLY ONE to whom any link with the masonic Hiram Abiff can be drawn." I find this odd because the one thing that I would have been sure this writer would have known well is the Bible text. Yet in the 2nd Book of Chronicles ch. 2 v. 13 I read in a letter from King Hiram of Tyre to Solomon:

"I am sending you Huram-Abi, a man of great skill" who has a father from Tyre and a Jewish mother just like the Hiram in 1 Kings ch. 7. In one sense it is true that there was no Hiram ABIFF because the latter part of this name was a Victorian misunderstanding of the Hebrew AVIV that meant 'of his father' whereas his real name was Hiram or Huram ABI. Nonetheless it is a mistake to say that there is no mention of this person in Scripture.

What IS legend, and is not in the Bible text, is the tale of the attack on this master mason/architect so that he suffers death rather than reveal the secret that he and two other Grand Masters shared between them, and then only when they met together. It so happens that it is whilst I have been writing this book that a researcher in medieval texts has directed attention to a French knightly tale that almost exactly reproduces the details of this incident in the Temple that must have been known to late medieval masons and adopted as the story of Hiram here. The fact is that Freemasons have always known and accepted as legend the 'murder angle' of this ceremony and it has never been claimed that this had the same authenticity as biblical events mentioned elsewhere.

There are serious questions that arise around reflection on the demise of this Hiram or Huram. It is among the first comment of the Worshipful Master that there occurs the term 'darkness visible', used by Fr. Hannah for his book, and this, the W.M. continues, 'is that mysterious veil which the eye of HUMAN REASON cannot penetrate, unless ASSISTED by that LIGHT which is from above'. Of the need of the biblical revelation to which every candidate is directed there is here no doubt. Here, we are reassured, 'the Lord of Life will enable us to trample the King of terrors beneath our feet, and lift our eyes to that bright Morning Star, whose rising brings peace and salvation to the faithful and obedient of the human race.'

"But who is the Lord of Life, or indeed the bright Morning Star?" asks John Lawrence. Well, one renowned Mason, Bro. Harry Carr, the secretary of the leading research Lodge in England, knew the answer very well. As a devout Jew he asked three of the Lodges to which he belonged to remove this paragraph from their ritual because it was obviously part of an earlier text that clearly referred to Jesus Christ and his resurrection. This, he knew, was spoken of in the Book of Revelation ch. 22 v. 16 where we read: "I, Jesus, am ... the Root and Offspring of David, and the bright Morning Star." What is surprising is the fact that during the last 200 years these words have been repeated in the Lodges of the world, including folk of various faiths, and yet the only direct objection to them that I have known is the one recorded above. For a Christian like myself it is just one more reassurance that deeply embedded in our Masonic practice is its Christian foundation. We shall yet see other examples of its presence.

In almost his last word on this degree John Lawrence writes: "This account shows how a RELIGIOUS Society can take a tiny passage from the Bible, about a relatively insignificant character, and elevate him to almost GOD-like proportions. He is known as 'Our Master' and in some ways is attributed with Christ's own life and actions."

Here again we have this author making statements that are without foundation. It was not a 'religious society' but a trade Guild Lodge that first fashioned the story of Solomon's Temple construction in the 17th century as part of a longer narrative. The whole tale covered God's creation of the world and his constant direction of it. It stretched from the first Adam to the second, Jesus Christ, and included many groups of triple characters some of whom we shall meet before this chapter ends. In no case, save one, could any of those persons be considered GOD-like and Hiram Abi has NEVER, in all my experience as a Mason, been so regarded. As an heroic man, perhaps, but never as even semi-divine. If this author detects in the 3rd degree story an intimation that might suggest that the principal character here represents Our Saviour Christ, is that good or is it to be dismissed? Here we again have the ambivalence: does John Lawrence want Freemasonry to be restored to a Christian enactment or does he, like many of the clergy, think that that would be encroaching too much on the Church's role? In any event, as we come later to the additional degrees, he may be in for a surprise.

It is at this point that I need to introduce a further portion of Masonic history as we start to deal with what was eventually called the Holy Royal Arch of Jerusalem. It is now evident, as was hinted above, that the essential core of this Order was present and known to Free and Accepted Masons by at least the late 17th century. It was not, as Fr. Hannah states in *Darkness Visible* (p. 154), "probably of more recent origin than the three Craft Degrees". As I have sought to show in my most recent book, *Royal*

Arch Journey, the newly devised 3rd degree of Master Mason of about 1726 was created from part of 17th century material reserved for Geometric Master Masons, who were men who had taken, or passed through, the Chair of a Craft Lodge. The insertion of what was called a CASUAL Master Mason degree BEFORE the Chair caused real disruption of Old St. John's Masonry. This led to some Masons being determined to preserve as much as possible of the original practice by insisting that access to the remainder of the Master's Part was to be restricted to those who had been installed in a Craft Chair. In 1834 all Master Masons were allowed to join the Holy Royal Arch, but occupying the chairs of the three Principals still required that one had to have been an Installed Master in the Craft. This Order was, as was clearly stated at the union of Grand Lodges in 1813, part of Ancient, i.e. pre-1717, Masonry.

The other preliminary note that is now necessary as I come to comment on the Holy Royal Arch is that several noticeable changes have been made in the ceremonies of this degree since Fr. Hannah made his comments in 1963. The three main changes are:

1. The removal altogether of the word JAHBULON from the ritual. It is never now used. The comments of a former Grand Secretary of the United Grand Lodge, when he was asked about this word, are as true still as they were then: "God is NOT referred to by that name … that word is an invention. It (was said to be) a description of God in 3 ancient languages. It is inaccurate scholarship but it's been existing in masonic ceremonial for some time. There is no attempt to unite gods of different religions and set that god up as a masonic god." (J. Lawrence, p. 101) I must say here that if there are any readers who would like not only more information about this discarded word but also the words used latterly in the third degree I will respond if they write to me privately.

2. On the top of the pedestal or double cube at the centre of the Chapter, which is what a gathering for the Holy Royal Arch is

called, there used to be three additional Hebrew letters that were said to refer to Father, Son and Holy Spirit. Since these could also be misunderstood they were removed and only the name JEHOVAH remains. For those unfamiliar with the way Scriptural names were composed, this latter name for God is the unpronounceable name JHVH with the vowels of the title AdOnAi (meaning 'My Lord') inserted.

3. There have been several omissions made in the three Lectures that have been delivered by the Principals since the alterations to the ritual in 1834. The historical lecture has dropped the dates previously mentioned in the light of more recent knowledge; the symbolical lecture has been shortened and simplified; whilst the mystical lecture has of course been shorn of the elements mentioned in points 1 and 2 above. I shall, therefore, refrain from commenting on anything Hannah and Lawrence say about the lectures unless it affects wording still retained.

There are two persistent matters that have increasingly exercised and concerned me in recent times. The first matter touches on the supposed objective of the Holy Royal Arch. This is expressed in the 2003 recommendations for changes in this Order as follows: "In the degrees which you received in your Craft Lodge you were taught that Freemasonry is a system of morality based on a belief in T.G.A.O.T.U. and giving brotherly love, relief and truth as the rule for your earthly pilgrimage" and there is a particular mention, as we have seen, of the Bright Morning Star's benefits for the human race ... However, it continues, "The Royal Arch develops this theme. It is therefore concerned with truth in the context of eternity and so leads its Companions to a higher understanding of the purpose of our mortal existence."

My concern with this elegant attempt to distinguish the Royal Arch from, but also show its connection with, the Craft degrees is that it does not highlight sufficiently the MORE THAN MORAL instruction of the first three degrees, nor does it explain sufficiently why and how this Order is not only desirable, but essential, for the completion of the Masonic journey.

Let me explain. Our religious critics have made much play with the fact that what Freemasons seem to be doing continually is stress the need for a moral endeavour which might eventually secure God's favour. I, on the other hand, have been stressing, on the basis of our ritual, that from the moment of our initiation we not only acknowledge the existence and the presence of God in our lives but our utter dependence on him and the need for his grace and guidance in our daily labour. It is easily forgotten that the First Degree Tracing Board is furnished with the symbols or persons representing Faith, Hope and Charity, which are the mainspring of whatever brotherly love, relief and truth we may display. This is made very clear in the 4th Section of the First of the appointed Lectures of the Craft where the ladder of Jacob at the centre of the Tracing Board is explained:

Q. Of how many staves or rounds was this Ladder composed?
A. Of many … but three principal ones, which are F., H. and C.

Q. Why Faith, Hope and Charity?
A. Faith in the G.A.O.T.U., Hope in Salvation, and to be in Charity with all men.

Q. I will thank you to define FAITH.
A. … We live and walk by Faith. By it we have a CONTINUAL ACKNOWLEDGEMENT of a Supreme Being. By Faith we have access to the throne of Grace, are JUSTIFIED, accepted and finally received…"

Q. HOPE.
A. Is an anchor of the soul, both sure and steadfast and enters into that within the veil. Then let a firm reliance on the Almighty's faithfulness animate our endeavours …

Q. CHARITY.
A. … It is the best and surest proof of the sincerity of our religion…'

How can anyone acquainted with such direction suggest that we need to be led, as in the Holy Royal Arch, to 'a higher understanding of our mortal existence'?

The fact is that as we know from a now much clearer knowledge of our historic past this Free and Accepted Masonry of ours was created from ONE DEGREE ONLY in which a mature man of faith, a Fellow, took a step of hope founded on a known God into a community of those who showed the Lord's charity. There was only one step more for our true forefathers to take and that was the entry, as a Master, into the inmost temple of the Lord's presence, which was considered a foretaste of eternity. That is why, to this day, the question is asked at the start of the incomplete Third degree, 'What inducement have you to leave the East and go to the West?' and the answer to which is there NEVER fulfilled. It is in the full Master's Part, now called the Holy Royal Arch, that the supreme quest is achieved and the Summum Bonum experienced.

That naturally introduces the other matter for our attention. Can we sensibly speak of the Holy Royal Arch being the completion of the present Third Degree? 'What is lost in the Third Degree,' say some, 'the genuine secrets of a Master Mason, is NOT what is found in the R.A.' That, I must admit, seems at first to be an extremely cogent argument until we look at the seeming problem from a historical point of view. If we were talking about work on a medieval building then there would be no doubt that the secret shared by any who were master masons would be that of the formula, with all the consequent calculations for creating a right-angled triangle, the basis of any building plan. Yet we are not here in that situation.

Once a Lodge became a Free and Accepted one certain other things of some consequence happened. The first was that though when only working stonemasons were involved no master mason was allowed into a lodge this changed when it became a Lodge that was attached to a Guild. The Guild was ruled by a Worshipful Master and two Wardens and so the Lodge steadily copied this pattern and the master masons now begin to have a place there. What in fact happened was that the term Master Mason begins to be applied to those who ruled a Lodge and, as had been the case with the master masons of old, these new Master Masons have a special 'secret' that they share.

The other change was that being aware of the nature of the Deity replaces the practical skill of planning a building. This was achieved by making the Master Mason secret that of emulating the plan of God the Creator. Being at first a fully Christian society the 'secret' was that of knowing 'the Father, the Son and the Holy Ghost'. From the 19th century onwards the name was JEHOVAH but, as with the Trinitarian sharing, three persons were required to share the NAME. If you therefore realise what a true Master Mason's word was meant to be then you can surely appreciate that this is not discovered in today's Master Mason Degree but is completed in the Holy Royal Arch.

There are two pieces of historical evidence that back up this explanation. We know that as early as 1730 not only was the idea of a Master Mason being the ruler of his Lodge recorded but, as is still the case in the Netherlands, a gold plate with the letters JHVH appears on the coffin of the dead Master Mason BUT it is NEVER explained. There was clearly more to be learnt. The other intriguing thing about English and Welsh Masonry is that for half my lifetime the Hebrew letters used on the pedestal in the Royal Arch were spoken of in the Mystical Lecture as 'Father, Son and Spirit'. Old traditions die hard.

Before we attempt to answer the concerns of Walton Hannah and John Lawrence about those parts of the Royal Arch not so far referred to there is one more historical point to be cleared up. For most of my own life as a Freemason I have been led to believe that this part of our history is either too mysterious or too complicated to be unravelled.

The usual explanation of its past has been that it was compiled either by Irishmen, or perhaps Frenchmen, in the period 1730–40 so that the first evidence of it is naturally about that time. As it was said not to have formed part of previous Freemasonry it was rejected by the premier Grand Lodge as of no standing or significance.

I have to declare that this is no longer the true story of this degree or Order and that what we have in what was LATTERLY called the Royal Arch is the re-appearance of what was once known as the 'Master's Part'. This was, as I have mentioned earlier, work restricted to whose who were true Geometric Master Masons who had passed through the Chair of an Accepted Lodge. We now call them Past Masters.

How then, the reader may well ask, did we arrive at the situation in which we now find ourselves? Now we have a Casual Master Mason degree, with only substituted secrets, and a Royal Arch Order that can be entered by a present Master Mason. However, it is still required that a Mason must have passed a Craft Chair to occupy the last two of the three Principals' Chairs. Although a full explanation is given in my new book mentioned above, I offer here a brief outline of the story because it relates to some matters referred to later in this book.

As the leaders of the 1717 Grand Lodge of London and Westminster began to grapple with the task of organising this new body it seems that they were either ignorant of, or just not interested in, certain crucial information. Central to this information was how the three degrees in ancient Freemasonry had been arranged. By 1700 it appears that the arrangement was for there to be a degree ceremony of Fellow before the Chair, and on the same evening a preliminary admission of an Apprentice if that step had not already been taken in the course of trade employment. That would obviously have been the case with non-operative members who were 'accepted' as Lodge Masons.

After these steps, taken before occupying the Chair, there was then a Master Mason step, also called the Master's Part. With the combined knowledge that we have of the content of the 17th century Old Charges and the revived St. John's Masonry ritual, called the Heredom of Kilwinning and revived in the 1730s, we can now attempt to construct the content of this Master's Part. The ritual of the Fellow degree, otherwise known as that of a Master craftsman or journeyman, concentrated, but not solely, on moral lessons symbolised by the tools and practices of a working mason. For a Master Mason there was a much grander design. It was nothing less than the recalling of the Creation of the world and memorising the doings of the 'architects' who obeyed God's directions in the constructing or managing of it.

Let us recollect here that that the very word 'architect' comes from "arché" = senior, first or head, and 'tectōn' = a skilled worker, and so, Master Mason. The story that was then restricted to the Chair degree was that of Adam and the Fall, the Flood, the Ark, the Tower of Babel, the Jewish emergence with Abraham, Moses and the Tabernacle, the kingdom with David and Solomon's Temple, the return from exile and building the temple of Zerubbabel, and the coming of the Messiah and the Last Judgement. It was in fact the retaining of the old Corpus Christi play cycle programme newly presented in a Bible, which was now translated into everyday English. This was, when you think about it, highly appropriate knowledge for the Masters of the original masons' trade. It was called the lectures or catechism of Harodim, or Master Overseers. It was also known as Noachic Masonry because of the part played by Noah in overcoming the Flood and the eventual redemption of the world by another Noah, Jesus Christ, through the waters of baptism. The possession of this knowledge in the wake of the Reformation was for long a truly great secret.

It only had one defect. It was a great deal to remember and learn. It is hardly surprising that by 1717 there were few who could recall such details. What is certain is that this was all meant to be the preserve of the rulers of a Lodge. By 1726 a section of this knowledge was extracted from the full story and made available to a new class of Masons called, incorrectly, Master Masons. 'Incorrectly', because they were not being put in possession of the whole 'secret' of what the rank of Master Mason entitled them to have. They just had the portion concerning Solomon and one other Master Mason, Hiram Abi. The remainder of the old knowledge, concerning the Tabernacle and the Second Temple, was now restricted to anyone who was through the Chair of a Craft Lodge, and it was given a new name, the Holy Royal Arch of Jerusalem. The need to have been through the Craft Chair was normally retained till 1834, after which any Master Mason was allowed to become a Chapter Mason.

In the light of this story it is not surprising that the present opening of a Royal Arch Chapter requires the naming of the sublime attributes of the Creator God of Scripture, and of the Qur'an, Omnipotent or All-powerful, Omniscient or All-knowing, and Omnipresent or All-encompassing. This is at once followed by the Anglican Collect for Purity, from the main act of worship in that Church. It is a prayer which fully presents the distinctive stance of the three great religions by addressing God face to face and that underlines the need stated elsewhere, that "by the inspiration of Thy Holy Spirit, … we may perfectly love Thee and worthily magnify Thy Holy Name." Lawrence complains that the ritual, "while omitting Christ's name as mediator, continues with the assumption that an individual can stand in innocence or purity by virtue of marvellous works or good conduct". (p. 100) Surely this is perverse. If God is to be known as the Trinity then the presence of the Holy Spirit replaces Christ in this instance, and there is surely enough admission of our need to be so cleansed, even in the thoughts of our hearts, that we may then, and ONLY THEN, love and magnify God's Holy Name?

In the light of what has just been explained it can be appreciated that whereas the original password into this Order was one known only to Past Masters it was, after 1834, necessary to devise a new word or form of words when Master Masons were admitted as candidates. Having taken advice from no less a biblical authority than the Chief

Rabbi in England the Duke of Sussex submitted the present words from the book of Hosea as the most appropriate. John Lawrence suggests that "In whatever way it is viewed it is very clear from the context that it refers to those with a special knowledge." While it may seem that Freemasonry is full of secrets which need to be revealed and, usually, reviled, I am sure that this is not the case here. The words 'AMMI RUHAMAH' were, as we have just stated, just a necessary replacement without any past Masonic significance. They were selected because they appeared in the same set of daily readings in a synagogue as applied to the other Chapter Bible extracts. Just as the Collect above was an authentic usage of one religious group, so this password was the same from another. There is no hidden agenda here.

The candidate is now invited to 'kneel and receive the benefit of Masonic prayer'. Let it be clearly understood that this does not imply that there is something exceptional, or specially distinctive, about the prayer to be offered. It is simply that this is prayer offered in a Masonic meeting. It is prayer to the God of Creation known in the Bible and once more there is a plea for 'a portion of Thy Divine Spirit' which, for myself, implies the Trinitarian God I acknowledge. What is undeniable is the statement with which this prayer ends: 'the object of our Institution is the welfare of our fellow-creatures, but, ABOVE ALL, the honour and glory of Thy most Holy Name'.

Why, John Lawrence wonders, does the candidate for this Order now have to enter blindfold when he has dispensed with that practice in his passage through the Craft? The fact is that though he is here embarking on what is the fulfilment of his Craft journey, it was once the preserve of true Master Masons who were rulers in the Craft. God is addressed now as the 'True and Living God Most High', which echoes countless verses in the Bible such as: "I cry out to God Most High, to God who fulfils his purpose for me" (Psalm 57 verse 2).

Moreover, the further point of the blindfold is indeed to emphasise that it is not by one's own effort that mankind attains the true knowledge of God, for 'by nature (one) is the child of ignorance and error'. It is only by 'the revelations of His Holy Will and Word' that one can be certain that true light is received. And to enable this wondrous thing to happen the new Companion is asked 'to wrench forth the Key-stone, and prepare to receive the light of the Holy Word'.

It is at this point that John Lawrence delivers one of his fiercest and most impassioned attacks on what is taking place. He says: "The corner – or keystone – of God's church is Christ (1 Peter 2:5–7). He is the most honoured and important part of the building. How it must break Christ's heart to see men who are called by his name involved in activity which removes him from his rightful place in order to establish another temple, this time made with human hands. The unwitting victim who symbolically casts aside the central stone, is acting out a blasphemous lie, an abomination of God's name and nature. This is spiritual wickedness and deception of the highest order, for the real secret that the candidate finds himself discovering is that of the ALLEGEDLY 'most sacred and mysterious name' of God signifying 'His Essence and Majesty Incomprehensible'." (p. 98) The writer is clearly very disturbed and troubled. The question here is: has he just cause for his deep feelings?

The first thing to be said from my own Christian view point is that we need to be quite clear about what the Bible says. What has to be realised is that whilst Christ is spoken of in Ephesians 2 and 1 Peter 2 as the chief CORNER-STONE, or head of the corner, of a building's foundation there is NO MENTION whatsoever of a KEYSTONE in Holy Scripture. Whilst I therefore fully understand the natural assumption that a head or cape-stone spoken of in Psalm 118, as that rejected of the builders, was a prophecy of Christ's rejection by the Jews, the mention in Zechariah 4 simply speaks of the capstone of the finished second temple being displayed by Zerubbabel, accompanied by the people's acclamation. To be strictly correct, therefore, the use of the term KEYSTONE in the ritual here refers, literally, to the central stone of an arch, which, I would suggest, is the proper use of it in such a degree as this.

Further, the stone is not here REJECTED but is just laid aside in order that the candidate might descend again to a place where he will find other words from the Bible to aid him in his search for God's truth. The accusation that what is taking place here is 'a blasphemous lie' is not only unproven but quite a hurtful slander.

This is made even clearer as we come now to the passage of Haggai's prophecy that the candidate hears read. Of this passage John Lawrence says: "Haggai's prophecy was originally given to encourage those engaged in the Temple's rebuilding after the exile in Babylon, but it looks beyond the physical building, to the complete and perfect fulfilment of GOD'S PLAN for HIS PEOPLE, both Jew and Gentile." Then, having so properly spelt out the fuller meaning of this historical event, which is acknowledged as part of the Bible, he goes on to add this: "The masonic ritual, however, lifts the VERSE into a FICTIONAL CONTEXT, where knowledge and morality, and not Christ are the key." (p. 98)

What exactly our author means by mentioning "the verse" or a "fictional context" I do not know. If he means by the former the reference to removing a keystone then I have tried to show that that does not carry the significance he is eager to suggest. If he is referring to the descent into a vault to discover a long-lost 'scroll or parchment' as fiction that is odd because even he remarks on the similarity of this tale to the Bible account of the rediscovery of the Law in the reign of King Josiah. There is also the early Christian excursion of Philostorgius who made such a descent into a vault to find a hand-written text of St. John's gospel. Indeed it is worth remarking here that up to 1834 the scroll found in the vault in this Order contained words from the start of John's Gospel ch. 1: "In the beginning was the Word and the Word was with God and the Word was God," which, though Christ was not mentioned, were clearly understood to refer to Him. After that date the first words of the whole Bible were substituted.

Even the discovery of these words from Genesis provokes criticism. They are spoken of as "part of the long-lost Sacred Law, promulgated by our Grand Master Moses", and the ancient tradition of making Moses part of the Masonic past is clearly a puzzle, if not an affront, to this clergyman. It may certainly be surprising to a new Freemason when he elsewhere hears that in the first official Constitutions of 1723 'Noah, Shem and Japheth' are spoken of as 'all Masons true' but that was how our forebears thought of them, as being upright forerunners of the Craft. If it is at this point, when John Lawrence is imagining that "knowledge and morality, and not Christ, is the key" that I can only turn to the ritual here which states: 'Let us therefore bless, praise, and magnify His Holy Name for the knowledge vouchsafed to us, and walk worthily in the light which shines around.' Any knowledge we have comes from God himself and the LIGHT is that which we also encounter in John ch. 1 v. 4 where we read: 'In him was life and that light was the light of men.' There can be no doubt for me whose light this is and who now calls me to walk in it.

More serious for John Lawrence is the suggestion that what the three Companions see on the top of the pedestal and beneath a veil "is more than was even revealed to Moses, or so it is alleged". (p. 99). Nowhere, that I am aware of, is anything so alleged but it may indeed be that when he and Fr. Hannah wrote their books there was a word, Jah-bul-on, that was pronounced by the Principals along with Jehovah. Never rightly explained, and open to serious misunderstanding, that additional word could, and did, give some cause for anxiety. I repeat that it has been, since their day, wholly removed from use.

John Lawrence also has a problem with the words used at the close of the ceremony regarding the retrieval of the 'genuine secrets'. These, we say, were recovered 'somewhat in dramatic form, the more forcibly to impress on your mind the providential means by which they were regained'. This author comments: "This statement is highly important. Not only does it indicate that freemasonry seeks to be self-authenticating, but also it is claiming specific divine intervention." (op. cit. p. 100) What puzzles me here is just what it is that seems unacceptable. Is it that Freemasonry should not attempt to explain how one of its practices came about, and if Freemasonry may not do so then who may? As for 'providential means', if such things are able to operate in other circumstances, as certainly they have in my own life, then why may they not be discerned in this instance? Do I detect here a wish to take any opportunity to find fault with this institution, however minor?

So we come to the latter part of this degree's work, the three Lectures. Nothing in the first or Historical lecture seems to have given any cause for concern and so we turn to the second or Symbolical one. Here there are two passages that need comment. The first of these has to do with the 'Supreme Being's powers of creation, preservation and annihilation'. Walton Hannah is convinced that this last power is a "purely Hindu conception that proved offensive to many" (op. cit. p. 175) Whilst it is certainly true that there is a Hindu Deity with destructive potentiality we must also wonder about the early view of the God of the Hebrews about which the author of Deuteronomy writes in, for example, ch. 9 verse 3: "But be assured today that the Lord your God is the one who goes ahead of you like a devouring fire. He will destroy them; he will subdue them before you, And you will drive them out and annihilate them quickly, as the Lord has promised you." Even as late as the compiling of the Psalms we have this in 145 v. 20: "The Lord watches over all who love him, but all the wicked he will destroy."

This is not a divine quality that we easily accept within a New Testament context but if, as our ritual creators seem to have done, you take a complete Bible background then this is seen as not merely a Hindu but a previous Hebrew description. I, as a Christian, might prefer not to have to acknowledge a part of my religious heritage such as this but if, as an ordained Anglican clergyman, I have publicly accepted the Bible as God's revelation then I cannot disavow it, even if I cannot easily explain it. Fr. Hannah and the Revd John Lawrence have to do likewise. What, for instance, would they make of our ritual if it included St Matthew 13 vv. 41, 42: "The Son of Man will send out his angels, and they will weed out of his kingdom everything that causes sin and all who do evil. They will throw them into the fiery furnace where there will be wailing and gnashing of teeth"?

Mention is made in this lecture of the stance adopted by the builders of the second temple who had the trowel in their right hand and their sword by their side. Traditionally the sword was said to be wielded in the left hand and that is why the sash with an aperture for the sword is on the right side of the body. The use of the left hand, symbolically armed with a sword to carry out the ancient penalty of this degree, then begins to makes sense, and the laying aside of a sword in order to make the formal toast to the 'Grand Originals' also explains why that is made with the left hand. These are not matters of deep belief but they are things that puzzle Companions and it is as well that we here take an opportunity to make sense of what we do.

In the Mystical Lecture John Lawrence reacted to the description of the sign of Reverence said to have been used by Moses at the Burning Bush. He objects to the words 'this sign was afterwards accounted unto him for righteousness' and continues: "This is a total distortion of fact since Moses' FAITH ALONE was counted to him as righteousness ..." (op. cit. p. 100) If his interpretation was correct then I would at once side with my fellow cleric but, again, he takes words out of their context and so he misunderstands them. The ritual here says: 'Moses, when the Lord appeared to him ... thus shaded his eyes from the brightness of the Divine presence, and placed his hand on his heart in token of obedience ...' The whole act is that of one who not only had faith in God but readiness to hear and do his will. The whole context is that God had chosen Moses to help and guide his people and, like Mary, the mother of Jesus centuries later, he was accounted righteous as he humbly accepted what was God's plan. It was not the sign of respect that EARNED or gained righteousness but his stance as a faithful servant that was taken account of by God. If you look at all the other Royal Arch signs they all express dependence on and trust in God, 'without whose Divine and special FAVOUR we must ever have remained unprofitable servants in his sight'.

John Lawrence ends his remarks on this Order with the following passage: "The whole degree ... thrives on vague doctrines of God, making him totally remote, while, at the same time exalting the brotherhood of man and human aspirations to immortality. The whole thing is summed up by the revelation explained by the Greek and Latin words on the breast jewel worn by all Companions "... on the triangle is inscribed EUREKAMEN Invenimus cultor dei civis mundi (we have found the worship of God, O Citizen of the world) ...' Need I say more."(p. 102) I always thought that 'cultor' was 'worshipper'.

The dots that close that quotation from our ritual do require that he should say or quote more if we are to get to the truth of all that we seek to do. Fr. Hannah does at least give us the rest of the passage so that we can appreciate the real understanding of this item: 'The Jewel which every Companion wears on his breast should inspire him with profound VENERATION for the Incomprehensible Being at whose command the world burst forth from chaos into light, and all created matter had its birth; whose Infinite WISDOM DIRECTS, and whose unspeakable Goodness PRESERVES and BLESSES every work that has PROCEEDED FROM His Hands.' Nothing could be clearer than this. Here is no mere 'human aspiration' but an undertaking directed by a wise and good Creator whose blessing pervades all that is done, and only such as is done, at his command. A Freemason who is truly and wholeheartedly seeking such direction has nothing to be ashamed of.

THE CHRISTIAN ORDERS

In the chapters that have preceded this, the reader will, I am sure, have begun to appreciate two undeniable facts about the development of what we know as English and Welsh Freemasonry today. The first is that for the first two and a half centuries of its existence the basis of what we call 'The Craft' was very clearly Christian. The second fact is that, reflecting the changing events that turned Britain into a worldwide, imperial power, Masonic ritual was amended so that men of different faiths might be able to share in the fellowship it offered. That is why there now appeared what must have seemed to be not only a non-Christian text but even an anti-Christian one. It is no wonder that John Lawrence could write this: "Concern from a Christian standpoint comes firstly from the fact that, certainly within CRAFT freemasonry, the masonry enjoyed by the bulk of the membership, Christ is EXCLUDED." (op. cit. p. 18)

This judgement is not, however, strictly fair. The truth is that it is DIRECT REFERENCE to Jesus Christ that is excluded, but the ritual still permitted a Christian interpretation by a believer of that faith. That, as has been said already, is a form of participation that was not only permissible and possible but was encouraged. The requirement that a Bible be open at all meetings, the emphasis on the need for God's grace, a continued use of the Lord's Prayer and the ample use of the term 'God' which, to a Christian, permits the sense of a Trinitarian Deity, were all elements that allow for the involvement of such believers as myself. Above all, the three knocks on the door of a Lodge, to ensure one's first admission, refer to the words of Jesus in Matthew ch. 7 verse 7: "Ask, and it will be given to you; seek, and you will find; knock, and the door will be opened to you." This is not all that could be said on this important point but is surely enough for the fair-minded questioner to accept as an assurance that the Christian basis of this Craft was far from ignored. Nor were the accompanying Christian 'intentions' of its members as they took part.

The truth is, however, that from the time after 1813 when this alteration took place there were many English Freemasons who were anxious about the future of certain ceremonies that they had already practiced since at least the 1770s. These included the Knight Templar and Knight Templar Priest Orders, the Red Cross of Constantine and St. John's Orders, and, not least, the Rose Croix of Heredom degrees. That these practices were even then not totally overlooked is proved by the attached wording to the Act of Union of the Premier and Antients Grand Lodges. It was there stated: "This Article (i.e. about Ancient Masonry) is not intended to prevent any Lodge or Chapter from holding a meeting of the Orders of Chivalry, according to the Constitutions of the said Orders." This statement reveals that other Orders had existed in a Lodge or Chapter setting and there is no intention of now excluding them.

As an indication of how Christian English Masonry had been I must mention an aspect that seems to have been totally overlooked by Hannah and Lawrence and yet was being practised in an increasing number of places in England when these two writers were making their attacks. This form of Masonry was evident in London in the late 1730s but seems to have been discontinued here when what we now call the Holy Royal Arch was being re-introduced by the Antients. As the Order was preserved north of the Border it now had the title 'Royal Order of Scotland' though its original name was 'Heredom of Kilwinning'. From quite a long ceremony it is difficult to choose just one portion but the following will have to serve:

Q. Worthy Senior Grand Guardian, since opening the Chapter what have we been doing?
A. Seeking a Word which was lost, and which by your assistance we have now found ...

Q. What for us did the Word?
A. Lived thirty-three years and a half upon earth, left a bright and shining example for us to follow, suffered a painful and

ignominious death for our salvation, and afterward ascended
into the Lodge of Heaven, where he continues with the
Holy Ghost to make intercessions for us with the Father,
Three Persons in One Godhead.

Moreover, this form of Masonry was re-introduced in the 1730s
because it was necessary to "correct the errors and reform the abuses
which had crept in among the three degrees of St. John's Masonry"
following the 17th century. It was so particularly clear a Christian
form of Masonry that the Duke of Sussex was obliged to modify it if
the Craft was to be established in the growing British Empire of the
19th century.

So determined was the Duke, however, on making sure that the
new United Grand Lodge had a firm start that he not only at first
overlooked the needs of the Holy Royal Arch but he sought to limit,
quite severely, the activities of the other Orders. He did this either by
being their chief officer, as in the Knights Templar and the Red Cross
of Constantine, or by his recommending other leaders to curb their
activities until the Craft had again settled down. It is important to
note that these Orders were by no means moribund or inactive and
this is the reason why, as soon as the Duke died in 1842, there was a
speedy reappearance of these Orders, admission to which required
that a Mason declare his acceptance of a Trinitarian belief. What is
revealed by the emergence of these additional degrees, 'additional'
because they were not 'higher', was a desire that the pre-Union basis
of English Freemasonry, as an essentially Christian movement, should
be re-affirmed.

There is also something else to note. Contrary to what has for long
been the idea that these Christian Orders were either distinct from, or
born out of other than, British roots the truth is that, apart from the
workings of the Rose Croix of Heredom, all the other ceremonies were
of British origin. These origins begin with being persons and incidents
recorded in the catechisms or lectures of earlier Masonic usage, or are

derived from a natural development of those elements. Thus, the Jewish builders of the second Temple under Zerubbabel, with a trowel in one hand and a sword in the other, eventually become symbolic crusading Christian knights in the Holy Land, whilst Bible-instructed Freemasons in Northern Ireland, pledged to support the British Crown, as they recalled the 17th-century rejection of the Stuart kings, become Knight Templar Priests. For fuller information about the way in which these and other Christian Orders evolved I would refer the reader to my book, *Delving Further Beyond the Craft*. What is most important to register is that we are not talking about mostly brand new Masonic practices such as are emerging in Freemasonry at the present time. These Christian Orders were very much part of our 18th century heritage and serve to underline the original overall Christian context in which the Craft then existed, as it did before that time.

Even with knowledge of that background and appreciating that there have always been many Masons in England and Wales who have cherished the Christian tradition of degrees, it is necessary for me to deal with some of the issues that still provoke doubt or displeasure for our Christian non-Masonic observers.

The Orders of Knights Templar and Knights of Malta have, as I stated earlier, attracted much attention in recent years, particularly as a result of such books as *The Hiram Key, The Second Messiah, The Bloodline of the Holy Grail* and *The Sword and the Grail*. Belief in the pretended medieval origin that they suggest is not one that the Brotherhood should encourage even though, as we shall see, there are traces of it in the Red Cross St. John degree.

Other than regarding the perambulations, holding a taper in one hand and a skull in the other, and fixing one's eyes upon the latter, as an exercise in the old practice of 'memento mori' – the proper recollection of one's mortality – Fr. Hannah comments that this is "comparatively innocuous and boyscoutish". For Freemasons who are no longer introduced to the display of the skull and crossbones in the Master Mason degree this may be a somewhat unusual experience but one that is not likely to be soon forgotten. The words with which the candidate is despatched on his symbolic 'year of penance' may be sober but yet full of promise: "rest assured that a firm faith in the truths revealed to us will afford you consolation in the gloomy hours of dissolution, and ensure your ineffable and eternal happiness in the world to come." We are in the realm of Romans 8 v. 11: "And if the Spirit of him who raised Jesus from the dead is living in you, he who raised Christ from the dead will also give life to your mortal bodies through his Spirit, who lives in you."

When we turn to the chivalric Orders of the Red Cross of Constantine, the Holy Sepulchre and St. John the Evangelist we encounter, says Fr. Hannah, ceremonies "concerned supposedly with the defence of the Christian faith as already delivered. They are therefore free from the HIGHLY OBJECTIONABLE characteristics of the Rose Croix of Heredom…" (op. cit. p. 199) We shall come to the matter of the Rose Croix shortly but there are certain points in the Red Cross and St. John ceremonies which claim our attention first.

After the initial ceremony of the Red Cross degrees in which a Mason who is both a Master Mason and a Royal Arch Companion is taught about the revelation of the Cross to the Emperor Constantine and his mother, Helena, we move on to two ceremonies, which underline the fully Christian character of pre-Union Masonry. The first of these takes place at the Sepulchre of Jesus and almost at once the Prelate begins to question the Prior and the other Officers about their duties. Of the Seneschal he asks:

'What is the chief defence of our Sanctuary?' and the reply is: 'It is the sword of the spirit, which is the word of God.' In complete silence and darkness a visitor is announced as: 'A Worthy Knight and soldier of the Cross who, having worked at the second temple and discovered the ANCIENT word, now prays … that he may learn the TRUE word of a Christian, and we discover that, as Christians, we progress from the ancient word to a further one here.

It now transpires that the knightly visitor comes from Bethlehem and his skill or 'art' is the building of 'Temples and tabernacles … in our hearts'. It is at this point that the Prelate informs the visitor that 'we are now in darkness and sorrow. The veil of the temple is rent; the cornerstone of our faith is overthrown; the Rose of Sharon sacrificed; the daystar of mercy obscured; and the TRUE WORD is lost.' To restore this loss there has to be a guard on the tomb and as that is being mounted three theological orations on Faith, Hope and Charity are given.

What is importantly taught in these addresses is that: 1. 'Faith is a firm conviction of the existence and attributes of God'; 2. Hope is 'based on the pure and active principles of Faith'; and 3. Charity is the heart reflecting 'a certain measure of the attributes of the great author of our being, and (so) bear the impress of the divine image'. The concluding words here are particularly significant and thus the more essential to be heard. 'Let us then carefully cherish and preserve the sacred flame which HIS GOODNESS has imparted and imitate, so far as human frailty will permit, His love, His compassion and His bounty towards the children of men. Thus, rising in the scale of moral excellence, the faithful Mason shall finally receive the crown of his labours, and be admitted into the assembly of the just made perfect, to that glory which fadeth not away.'

What is most noticeable is that nowhere here is there an emphasis simply on Christ as the only source and defining factor of 'moral excellence', and yet what is taught is indubitably Christian. Remember, I ask the reader, that this is ritual from before the Union, carefully preserved, and this, therefore, represents the character of that same Masonry that has been criticised for seeking to attain moral ends WITHOUT the acknowledgement of Christ. Here it is God, 'the author of our being', whose divine Spirit is to assist and direct us. If that is acceptable to these critics here where is the justification for their dismay at what seems like the absence of the second Person of the Trinity earlier? This is a issue that any who adopt their approach have, from their side, to answer.

What is now to be noted, as the degree of the Holy Sepulchre moves towards its culmination in the degree of St. John the Evangelist, is that certain distinctive phrases begin to be employed, such as: 'the day-star of mercy is obscured and darkness covers the earth … our temple is rebuilt; the cornerstone of our faith is restored; the daystar of mercy reappears in greater splendour and the word of God is found'. These are terms that we will see paralleled elsewhere before this chapter ends.

At this point of the proceedings the candidate is told that he 'will gaze for the last time upon the fragmentary forms and types of the Mosaic dispensation and return to us with the holy doctrine of the great evangelist, St. John'. There is now an entry to a vault where the Gospel of John is found, and we hear the words: '… the Book declared that he who had uttered this was God, the Creator of all things'. There follows the recitation of the legend of the degree and it is in the course of this explanation that some striking words are used. 'The symbolic mystery of Hiram's death represents to us that of the Messiah' and the very core of what is being done is expressed thus: '… the grand mystery of Christian Masonry is a sincere belief in Jesus – the Lamb of God'. Is it any wonder that, as John Lawrence said much earlier, Hiram "is known as 'our Master' and in some ways is attributed with Christ's own life and actions". (op. cit. p. 92) For that idea to be openly declared in Craft Masonry after the Union of 1813 was not acceptable. For the Christian Mason it is the unexpressed, but constant, confirmation of his right to belong to this Society.

If our critics endorsed the Knight Templar and Red Cross ceremonies they were far from happy with those of the Rose Croix of Heredom, otherwise known as the 'Ancient and Accepted Rite'. John Lawrence has at first partly made his view clear but on p. 108 of his book he lists his concerns more fully and I will reproduce them all before I offer some reply:

1. He questions the description given here of the day of Christ's death. 'Since masonry has experienced such dire calamities, it is

our duty, Princes, to endeavour by renewed labours to retrieve our loss …' How could such a day be a calamity?

2. 'If this is to be equated with Christian doctrine, then it must be freely available to all. The gospel is not something to be kept deliberately secret.'

3. 'Salvation, it is clearly implied, is dependent on the discovery of the word, it does not come through faith in Christ … knowledge of information is not God's way to eternal life.'

4. 'The masonic communion is far from scriptural, merely taking the elements and using them in a most indiscriminate way. There is no attempt at consecration.' What are we now to believe, he asks, about the earlier claim that Masonry has no doctrine or Sacraments?

5. The American Masons say that unless this Order can be enjoyed by those of ALL religions it cannot be part of Freemasonry.

These are significant points and are found to be even further stressed by the comments of Fr. Hannah. In *Darkness Visible* he says: "The most deadly heresy of this degree lies in the fact that it is the Candidate himself who symbolically achieves both light and perfection by his own efforts, not in Christ or Christ for him. It is the Candidate who gives his age as thirty-three, who journeys for thirty-three days, passing through the Black Room and Chamber of Death to his mystical resurrection in the Red Room … And the Resurrection in the closing ceremonies is defined significantly as 'the hour of the Perfect Mason'. Our Lord's redemptive death is treated as a type and an allegory of the experiences that a Mason must undergo in the quest for light, not as a unique and objective act of redemption wrought for him by God. That is, of course, a purely Gnostic conception."

All this sounds most impressive and convincing, but wasn't the candidate a declared believer in the Holy Trinity before he was admitted?

And what about the help of the New and Better Covenant on his travels for which we have twice prayed? Moreover, at no point is the candidate ever informed that he is impersonating Christ or that he has passed through a Resurrection. That may be our critic's interpretation but it is not borne out by the ceremony to which he refers.

Fr. Hannah further quotes as follows from the ritual: "the Rose is an emblem of secrecy and silence; in the Song of Solomon we find reference to the Saviour under the mystical title of The Rose of Sharon". 'Here indeed', he writes, 'in this direct association of Christ with an emblem which (according to Masonry, not the Bible) signifies secrecy, is a further admission that this degree interprets Christianity in the light of a mystery-religion of the type abhorred and anathematised by the early Church.' (op. cit. pp. 206, 207) I shall comment on the Rose theme shortly.

Finally he comments on the closing ceremony of this degree that is known as the Third Point or Feast of Fraternal Affection. He writes: "though outwardly professing to be a mere AGAPE or love-feast, (this) has in its close context with Calvary a possible interpretation far more sinister. A wafer is first consumed" after dipping in salt. The presiding officer, here called 'The Most Wise Sovereign', then presents his neighbour with the chalice of wine and the word 'Immanuel' (God with us) and this is acknowledged by the neighbour saying the words 'Pax vobiscum' (Peace be with you). When all have shared the Sovereign then says 'All is consumed' to which reply is made 'Gloria in excelsis Deo et in terra pax hominibus bonae voluntatis (Glory be to God on high and peace to men of good will).'

If all these severe judgements are indeed provable or fair then the 50 years that I have belonged to this Order, as in so many others, must have been misspent and squandered. It is because I am utterly convinced that this is not the case that, at the risk of wearying the reader, I must now answer every one of the points made by these ordained colleagues.

The first point that is made is that what we call Good Friday can hardly merit the description that we have here and in the Order of the Red Cross. As a point of departure what did the disciples think about the events of that day? Was it not such a day of horror and disbelief when such things could happen to their leader, Jesus? The gospel writers give us a selection of impressions that, put together, exactly fit the words at the start of this degree:

"Now from the sixth hour there was darkness over all the land till the ninth hour ... Jesus, when he had cried again with a loud voice, yielded up the ghost. At that moment the curtain of the Temple was rent in twain from top to bottom. The earth shook and the rocks rent." (Matthew 27 vv. 45, 50, 51; Mark 15. vv 33–41; Luke 23 v. 44).

There is no direct reference to the cubic stone in the Bible but John Lawrence has already made ample reference to this item as descriptive of Christ and for Freemasons this is the perfect ashlar. In the palace of the Escorial close to Madrid there is a mural in its library, which depicts Christ sitting on a white cubic stone below a rainbow. You can hardly have a more defining identification than this in what is a Catholic setting even though the idea of the Cubic Stone was a Rosicrucian one ... And it is in John 19 v. 34 that Christ has "his side pierced ... and forthwith there came out blood and water". The Blazing Star is a reminder of that first herald to the shepherds and wise men of a newborn Saviour whose life and ministry now seem eclipsed.

Of course this momentous day is no longer regarded by Christians as a day of calamity but that is with the gift of hindsight and in the wake of Easter Day. What is important is that in the midst of the disciples' despair and tribulation God is still in control. We therefore pray to Him with the Anglican collect for the 14th Sunday after Trinity and ask HIM to give us "the increase of Faith, Hope and Charity" and that we may "love that which THOU dost command". Where does Fr. Hannah get the idea from that a candidate is to achieve his goal simply "by his own efforts"? At once, in the opening ritual, we have this prayer: 'Save, we beseech Thee, O God in Heaven, Creator and

Sovereign of all things, us Thine UNWORTHY children.' Does not the Lord in heaven include Father, Son and Holy Spirit?

John Lawrence's second point is that if what we have been dealing with in this degree is true Christian doctrine then why should we "treasure (it) up in the secret repository of our hearts"? Surely we should want to proclaim it abroad? But wait a minute. Are you now wanting Freemasonry to be some sort of evangelising agency or would that not be attempting to be a sort of church? In any case do you proclaim your heart-felt beliefs in the golf club, at the bridge table, in the pub or at a soccer match? All that is being recommended at the end of our ceremonies is that we do not forget what we have learnt, promised and undertaken to do, as and when it is appropriate. There is no 'deceit' or 'undercover activity' in prospect. We just need to hold spiritual lessons dear.

The third point is a crucial one. "Recovering the Word" is not a matter of just receiving information. It is the fresh discovery of what is the most important thing in my, or anyone else's life. It is being one of the disciples on the road to Emmaus and finding that our companion is the Word of whom the gospel writer John speaks: "In the beginning was the Word and the Word was God … And the Word was made flesh and dwelt among us." (John 1 vv. 1, 14) It is no less than that discovery in the Red Cross that 'the grand mystery of Christian Masonry is a SINCERE belief in Jesus – the Lamb of God'. (see p.68 above). I would have thought that in these days a society that had at its core a reminder of the whole Easter story would be a body that the Church would value – not demean.

The fourth point, about a so-called 'Masonic Communion', is obviously one that both these clergy critics relish. What disturbs me about the comments now made is that whereas they have in most cases elsewhere taken exception to what is said as being unscriptural, they now take exception to what is NOT said. I suggest that a fair-minded reader would appreciate knowing what is really done and said.

The members, known as Princes, stand in a CIRCLE into which a new member is formally admitted, and the circle is described as an emblem of Eternity. So assembled, the Sovereign says: "Princes we now invite you, according to Oriental custom to break bread and eat SALT with us." It should be noted that from the outset there is no suggestion of a similarity with any celebration of a communion service. Standing in a circle, always in my experience breaking hard water biscuit, not bread and certainly not a 'wafer', and dipping it in salt, surely mark the distinction. There is no mention of, or intention to, commemorate the Last Supper for this is simply a fraternal, if sincere, 'pledging to each other our fidelity and friendship in the GOBLET of fraternal affection'. You should note that we use no 'chalice' but a secular drinking vessel, and so that we have no doubt as to where the source of our true living lies, the invitation continues. 'Let us invoke the blessing of Him who is the Rose of Sharon and the Lily of the Valley, by WHOSE ASSISTANCE we hope to progress here on earth TOWARDS that perfection which can be consummated ONLY, when, rising from the tomb, we ascend to join our great Emmanuel and are united with Him for ever in a glorious and happy Eternity.'

The Rose and the Lily again mentioned here have no reference to secrecy but have their ancient symbolic allusion to the Virgin Mary or her offspring, Jesus. Here, then, is the very connection with Christ, as in the Second Point of the ceremony, which our critics are seeking and what is more we here declare that not only is our perfection as persons unattainable without such assistance but it will not be ours until we share the power of the resurrection that he has prepared for us. Here may I just add that in the journey made by the candidate up to this climax Fr. Hannah emphasises the achieving of light and perfection by his own efforts. Why, then, does the Sovereign say to the candidate as he travels: 'I particularly commend to your meditation the beauties of the New and Better Covenant (that is the New Testament) and that you may more completely appreciate its excellence, let us invoke GUIDANCE and DIRECTION FROM ABOVE.'

The fifth point raised by John Lawrence is that made by our American Brethren who think that such sublime Masonry requires that all should be able to share it. Here I, as a Christian, have to declare that I am reassured by the Supreme Council's long-standing decision for England and Wales that this was, is and will remain a prerogative for Christians only as in our pre-Union practice. That is because our controlling body knows how truly consonant with Christianity this degree is.

There was one matter which I must confess surprised me in Fr. Hannah's comments. He speaks of the Prelate formally committing the four letters of the Sacred Name, I.N.R.I., to the flaming container and using the words 'consummatum est'. It is because others beside this cleric misunderstood the Latin that they are now rendered in English. The Latin words meant that Christ's work was accomplished, or as his words from the cross are recorded, "It is finished," and so had nothing to do with anything being consumed. It is to be hoped that when Fr. Hannah joined the Roman Communion he had a revision course in the language that that Communion still used.

Nothing is therefore more fitting as we come to the end of this chapter than to dwell for a few moments with the closing ceremony of this Ancient and Accepted Rite. Here we pick up the same components as in the Red Cross. The Word is found, the Blazing Star reappears, the clouds of darkness are dispersed and the message of St. John 'to love one another' is reinforced. Above all, as Christian Masons, we are again charged 'to erect an edifice in our hearts to the Glory of the Lamb' – so here is Christ – 'to whom belongeth Might, Majesty, Dominion and Power, Who liveth and reigneth world without end'. Is this so improper a place for a Christian who is a Mason to be?

OTHER ADDITIONAL DEGREES

We now need to turn to certain additional degrees that are mentioned by Fr. Hannah and the Revd John Lawrence. These are mostly parts of English and Welsh Freemasonry, which any Mason who has the necessary qualifications can join. Having been a member of these degrees for 50 years and having been given the privilege of high rank in each of them, I trust that the reader will believe me when I say that not only do I know a good deal about their workings and history but I have valued the lessons which each of them has taught me.

I begin this part of my story with Mark Masonry. Today a candidate is admitted to what seems to be a single degree but originally there were two. The first degree, attached to the Fellowcraft, was called the Mark Man, whilst the second, which was conferred on Master Masons, was called that of Mark Master Mason. Nowadays the two are given together and only to Master Masons.

The ritual of this degree relates to the imminent completion of the building of King Solomon's Temple. "The object of it is a search for 'the most important stone in the building' and focuses on Psalm 118 v. 22 which reads 'the stone that the builders rejected has become the head of the corner'. Having found the stone, the promise of Revelation ch.2 v. 17 is read out, 'To him that overcometh will I give to eat of the hidden manna and I will give him a white stone and in the stone a new name written which no man knoweth saving he that receiveth it.' John Lawrence continues: "In this country the degree is open to anyone professing to be a Christian, which probably means the vast majority of the population." (op. cit. p. 103) From that last remark the reader will not be surprised that this work was written over 20 years ago.

There are some inaccuracies or misunderstandings in the above description. The first is that this degree has never been restricted specifically to Christians, whether nominal or otherwise, and Jewish

Brethren, in particular, have always been keen devotees of the Mark. That is why Fr. Hannah wrote, "The Mark degree is no more Christian than the Craft. It can be allegorised in a Christian direction only by misunderstanding the exclusive character of Christianity, the uniqueness of our redemption in Christ, and the true meaning of faith." (op. cit. pp. 197ff) In one sense this pair of degrees could have been seen in a Christian setting because they emerged from the lectures of pre-Union practice, and also if you interpret the stone rejected in this degree as representing the expected Messiah.

Where a problem arises is, as we saw in the chapter on the Holy Royal Arch, when we confuse the 'keystone' here in the Mark, the pivotal item of an arch, with biblical reference to a 'cornerstone, headstone of the corner, or coping stone to finish off a building'. The two are not interchangeable and once you acknowledge this then any attempt at identifying the stone that is rejected as Christ collapses. The only small resemblance is that the keystone, even as a breast jewel, is, as mentioned in Revelation, WHITE. John Lawrence quite correctly adds: "the symbolism is very strange indeed, far from consistent with orthodox Christianity". (op. cit. p. 104) This final comment is hardly surprising in view of what has been said already. The symbolism has at least two very pertinent lessons to teach us. The first is that God, the Great Overseer, does 'mark' what we do with our lives and whether we make a worthy mark on what we undertake. The second is that we do well to learn that we do not always get what we deserve or what we think others should do for us. Rejection should not lead us to dejection or bitter regret but to a renewed dedication in the future. That is why the older version of the story as it is recorded by Fr. Hannah is better as a lesson than what we now have.

Attached to the Mark degrees there is a ceremony that is known as the Royal Ark Mariner. Fr. Hannah dismisses it as "distinguished only by its trivial silliness.' John Lawrence remarks that "the ritual is a concoction of biblical fact and masonic fiction. It is arguably more

Christian than Mark Masonry but is again not seen as exclusively Christian elsewhere in the world." (op. cit. p. 104)

I have again to remark that this has never in my experience been regarded as restricted in membership and its originally strong Christian association has long since been forgotten. What does reveal the earliest Christian context of not just this degree, but a whole NOAH, or Noachic, section of the first catechism of our Craft, are two features. The first of these is the exclusion of Ham, the eldest son of Noah, from the Masonic scene and that was a decision based on medieval Church teaching about him. The second feature is that Shem thus becomes the prime member of the brothers and it is from Shem that in due course Jesus Christ descends. (See Luke ch.3 v.36). None of this is now mentioned or known by candidates for the degree, much less by others. If anyone wants to pursue this fascinating pathway in early English Freemasonry they should consult my *Arch and the Rainbow* (pp. 318 ff).

We now turn to a series of five degrees called 'The Allied' by Masons today. These five separate ceremonies are a residue of pre-Union attachments to other parts of our whole Masonic programme as largely set out in the 18th century lectures. I say 'largely' because, in fact, the first of these degrees has a peculiar and distinct history. The degree of St. Lawrence the Martyr was in fact a degree appendant to that of a Fellow or Master craftsman just as much as an Apprentice one was at the start of the 18th century. This degree was introduced in order to prove the status of operative masons in an Accepted Lodge. This was a practical measure because operative masons did not have to pay the same fees as candidates who were not of the mason trade, as well as being exempt from taking an Apprentice step. The degree seems to have been based upon a well-known medieval tale of how the Saint was tortured on a hot gridiron after refusing to surrender the 'treasures' of the Church in his care. These 'treasures' were in fact the local poor and orphans, but his captors thought he was concealing actual riches. Those wanting to read more about this fascinating sideline of early Masonry should read my book on *Delving Further Beyond the Craft*. What I should say here is that when this incident was used as a late medieval Saint's play in Beverley, Yorkshire, it was the masons who acted it to represent Charity overcoming the sin of Avarice.

It has always, to my knowledge, been understood that this degree, like the rest of the Allied series, was open to Masons of any faith. On that understanding it was suggested, some thirty years ago, that a Jewish Brother, an Assistant Provincial Grand Master no less, would find new interest and a new circle of acquaintances by taking these degrees. After taking the St. Lawrence degree, and to my astonishment, he said that he could not, on faith grounds, go on with this part of Masonry because it centred on a Christian Saint, and, so far as he could now see, would involve him next time in a ceremony that touched on Constantine who became a Christian and those who were presumably Christian knights. In this latter assumption he was mistaken, but for him the St. Lawrence experience was enough. In terms of understanding the real and intimate links between Belief and Brotherhood this experience was a necessary lesson. To me the degree is just about greed, wrong judgement, the burden of misunderstanding, and charity. To Bro. Asher it was a subtle inference of the superiority of Christian behaviour.

It is a pity that Bro. Asher did not pursue the rest of the Allied list because as a keen Royal Arch Mason he would have been fascinated to learn the secrets of the Grand High Priest which were once conferred on the holder of the Chair of Most Excellent Zerubbabel. For those who might like to savour a little more of what were the rich tributaries of 18th-century Freemasonry that can complete the story of the Solomonic Temple and the Babylonian exile, the next two of the Allied series have their special interest.

This is no less true of the so-called Cryptic degrees that are so named because they describe events concerning an underground chamber, crypt or vault in which matters relating to the Holy Royal Arch are revealed. Again, persons of any faith are able to share in these ceremonies but a candidate has had to become a Mark as well as a Royal Arch Mason to be admitted.

I have attempted in my previous books to explain how it was that out of the association of those who were operative or working and trading masons there arose a society made up mostly of those not engaged in that trade. What I have also tried to do is to explain why there was eventually a decisive separation between the operative and Accepted Masons. This was because in several parts of the country in the late 17th century the mason trade so revived after the restoration of the monarchy that the working masons in these places asked their local authorities for a new charter since their previous company had been taken over by non-working members. Though the new charters usually required association with allied trades such as bricklayers, blacksmiths or paviors, they were granted and the separation of operatives and Accepted Masons began.

It was this separation that led eventually to a person, who had been admitted to the working trade but was also an Accepted Mason, forming the idea of introducing for Freemasons what was called an Assemblage of Operative Masonry. The detail of how that organisation developed is a story for some other place but in terms of what can be joined by men of any faith this is one of the most intriguing. Certainly, for anyone wanting to know how many of the symbolic items and movements of Accepted Craft Masonry originated, this is the body to join for though it was probably only formed in the 19th century it draws on true matters of operative practice. When he comments on not only most of the degrees just mentioned, but also the Orders of Women's Freemasonry, Fr. Hannah says that they are "mostly convivial, partly moral, but devoid, to the best of my knowledge of any speculative, philosophical, Biblical or religious content. Some of them, however, claim a considerable antiquity." (op. cit. p. 209)

It is in regard to the matter of speculative or philosophical content that I have kept back to this point mention of the Societas Rosicruciana In Anglia. In this Order there are nine degrees and of them Fr. Hannah writes as follows: "Although open only to Master Masons these degrees are quasi-Masonic and are completely different in tone from any regular Masonic system. The rituals of the various degrees are frankly theosophical and pseudo-rosicrucian, and are an extraordinary hotchpotch of high-sounding oriental mysticism and sham occultism. Very surprisingly, these degrees are alleged to be for Christians only" and "Closely associated with the S.R.I.A. is the Order of Eri." (op. cit. p. 208) For a selected few, from the latter step it is not far to the modern equivalent of the Hermetic Order of the Golden Dawn.

First of all it is surprising to me that the degrees of the S.R.I.A. are not open to men of any faith, for the scope of study encouraged by the devoted leaders of this segment of Masonry is such as to benefit from those of other faiths. It is equally surprising to me that our two Christian critics, in pursuit of dubious Masonic participation in various parts of Freemasonry by Christians, should not have highlighted parts of these rituals that might have been rather more proper for their attention than their choice in the Craft and Royal Arch degrees. Readers may notice that I have delayed mentioning the S.R.I.A. until this point and that is really because I do now believe that anyone with strong Christian convictions may do well to enquire carefully of those already in the S.R.I.A. as to whether this is something that can properly deserve his attention.

Undoubtedly there are features of the S.R.I.A. that reflect some of the great historic episodes in the path of seeking knowledge and wisdom, and the initial step of Zelator is one that captures the imagination. Yet that is but the start of a quite long journey that can take an 'adept' along surprising pathways. It is true that there is the constantly renewed invitation to members to contribute their private study and insights for the benefit of each College, but the opportunity to study sufficiently to offer a continual stream of worthwhile addresses is not one that many seem to have. What is certainly commendable is the effort to stimulate exchanges of views by the members, but the wide range of subjects that can be presented means that only a few can usefully participate whilst others may be out of their depth. What is also true, in what is claimed to be a Christian membership, is that the range of discussion can extend into some of the areas referred to by Fr. Hannah. If anywhere in the wide landscape that is modern Freemasonry there might be an area entitled 'Take care' it is here that a Christian Mason might find himself to be.

I have perhaps, in this chapter, opened up for some Freemasons vistas that they have not previously considered or even known about. As in the earliest days of one's engagement in the Craft, the advice to weigh up sensibly the time, effort and resources that one can devote to Masonry's various orders is particularly appropriate when one has to choose between a degree that has retained its Christian format and one that is applicable to all men, or women, of faith. For some Masons that is not a choice that is relevant and we should rejoice that there is much to be enjoyed that does not have to be judged by Christian standards. My own experience has been that every degree can to a surprising extent enhance the faith that one already possesses and enrich that faith by pointing the way to the right behaviour of any man or woman.

SOME ISSUES OF FAITH

In the course of writing this book there are three things that have been repeatedly referred to as matters of major concern by Christian critics of the Craft. The first is the exclusion of the name of Jesus Christ in prayers, promises and parts of the ritual. The second is the apparent danger of syncretism through association with people of other faiths in such a setting as a Lodge. And thirdly, there is the specific issue as to whether it is more serious for a bishop or priest to be a Freemason than for a layman. Though partial answers to these matters have occurred in the foregoing chapters I think it is necessary to deal with them as fully as I can before this book ends. I must also take this opportunity of speaking about what I can only call the 'doubtful step of double standards'.

I make no excuse for amplifying anything I may have said previously about what our clergy critics have called the "exclusion of Christ" from some of our Masonic ritual. I have, I hope, partially explained why there was at the start of the 19th century an attempt to take account of what were different and developing circumstances on the world scene. In the 17th and 18th centuries members of English or North American Lodges were those, Jews and Christians, who could accept the whole Bible story and acknowledge Jesus of Nazareth as a Jewish Rabbi. The gratitude of Jewish Masons at being accepted into some part of society on an equal footing was sufficient to outweigh the still traditional ways of Christian praying and speaking.

By the start of the next century the situation was needing attention. Of course it would have been possible to regard Free and Accepted Masonry as a merely British Islands phenomenon and to have left it as it was in 1800. That was no longer an option because the growth of the colonies and the extension of royal rule was accompanied by a shift in the way English and Welsh Freemasonry was now organised. The problem of two English Grand Lodges was now solved and in view of the many situations overseas, where relations with Irish and Scottish Masons had to be resolved, the Union of 1813 was a most necessary step. That at the same time there should be a resolution of the nature of the basic Masonic steps from Entered Apprentice to Holy Royal Arch was equally essential. If Freemasonry was to be part of the British heritage to be shared from Cardiff in Wales to Christchurch in New Zealand then it had to be adapted in the manner with which we are fully familiar.

What I am now utterly convinced of, and what I am no less sure was in the mind of that Christian peer, the Duke of Sussex, was that whilst it might SEEM that a distinctive Christian quality was absent because the specific mention of Jesus Christ is omitted, the tenor of the prayers, the constant turning to God for help and direction, and not least the call for the aid of the Holy Spirit, amply supply the devout Christian Brother with enough evidence that he is not in the wrong place. After all, who was it that Jesus himself prayed to, called on and pointed others to, during his earthly stay? Surely it was GOD the Father and we cannot be putting a foot wrong if we do what Christ did when he shared our flesh?

It is here that I think I should share with the reader a singular set of circumstances that I believe were providential. After some 18 years as a parish priest I was offered an opportunity to serve in what was then the oldest ecumenical organisation in Britain. This was the Conference of British Missionary Societies, which was founded in 1910. This gave me an entrée into every denomination except that of the Roman Catholic Church and by the time I left that post two bodies concerned with Mission even in that Church had also begun to take a part in some of our joint planning. It was through this involvement that I was invited to become General Secretary in the British and Foreign Bible Society, the oldest Bible Society in the world, having been founded in 1812. This had as its objective the provision of the Old and New Testaments in as many languages as the churches in different places require and the Society could afford to provide from donations.

This was, I am sure you may agree, a very suitable job for a Christian Freemason, and you may imagine my delight when I learnt that the Duke of Sussex, at the time of the Union of Grand Lodges and after, was one of the Presidents of this same Society. Not only so but it was his decision that led to the Annual Meeting of the Bible Society (as it is now called) being held on United Grand Lodge premises in Great Queen Street for fifteen years until the Society had its own building. This was because, whilst the Duke did not want the Craft to be identified with just one Church, he was happy for it to accommodate a Christian, biblical organisation. I never sit in a Lodge and Chapter, with the Bible open before us, without thinking of that singular arrangement. What that arrangement implied was that the Duke had no idea of removing the whole Bible message from the English Craft. If the God of the Bible is, as I and so many other Masons believe, Father, Son and Holy Spirit, then the absence of Christ's name is not, of itself, proof that some of us as Masons are disavowing the Trinity.

It is appropriately at this point that I turn to the issue of 'deism' and 'syncretism'. In a book from which I have so far not quoted, as it mostly repeats what has been stated by our two other critics, J. W. Acker of the Missouri Lutheran Church, says this: "In short, the Masonic concept of God is … 'Any God will do'. Now, if this view of God is permitted to permeate the church, and its members are allowed to subscribe to such a notion of God in becoming members of the Masonic fraternity, the church, to be consistent, should abandon all mission work, especially in foreign fields." (*Strange Altars*, 1959. pp 32f)

Again, as I have said previously, if this was really the case when people attend Masonic meetings then I would have long ago handed in my resignation. When faced with such a view the key to an answer is to have it clearly understood where we are when this kind of theologising is taking place. If we were in a town hall meeting, the local Rotary club, or at a regimental reunion there would not,

I suspect, be any suggestion that, although I would be mixing with people of various faiths or none, I would not be having my belief in God in any way jeopardised. Yet at all these gatherings there would be, as in a Masonic meeting, someone who said Grace, gave an opening prayer, or asked for prayers for some sick acquaintance. Why is attendance at such gatherings as these not regarded as likely to harm or tarnish the faith of the Christians present when they obviously think that that is what would happen in a Lodge?

The answer, I suppose, is that, for what they regard as very good reasons, a Lodge meeting has the reputation of being some kind of religious assembly. That a Lodge has such an air of spiritual activity about it is something for which Masons ought surely to be thankful but not, of course, if its activity is thought by recognised religious bodies to be some kind of rival competitor for members or a seed-bed of false teaching. What surprises those Freemasons who are themselves devout and devoted believers in their own places of worship, is that any outsider should imagine such a thing to be possible.

What is the most hurtful thing for a Brother such as myself to grasp is that anyone could imagine a Lodge replacing one's church or that just because I regularly meet, talk, act and eat with people of another faith than my own that can in any way affect, weaken or alter my own religious convictions. What is made abundantly clear from the very first moment that we agree to join this Brotherhood of Masonry is that neither matters of faith nor views on political matters are to be discussed or examined on the occasions that we meet in a Lodge. The idea that a man's or a woman's views in these areas can be affected, let alone tainted, by sharing in Masonic ceremonies is simply not true. My views in the religious sphere are as strong and personal today as they were when I joined a Lodge 60 years ago.

But what about those Masons who say that being in the Craft is their religion? Surely that means, our critics might say, that there is something in what you Masons do or teach that is different from what is done and taught in a place of worship elsewhere? Clearly I have no right to judge another Mason's position when we are together as Brethren. In general, however, and speaking as an individual in society, I believe that such a view as that above suggests too weak a religious commitment elsewhere before he joined and a real question as to whether such a person knows what religion is meant to be. Our United Grand Lodge has repeatedly stated that "Freemasonry is not a religion nor is it a substitute for religion." If that is correct, as I have certainly found it to be, then what a man or woman may appreciate about being a Freemason may be many things but it cannot provide what a valid religious commitment can offer. The Brother who still claims that being a Freemason is his religion just does not understand to what he belongs.

It is against that background of proper understanding that I turn now to the third issue of this chapter. Whatever is it that has led in the course of my lifetime to a serious drop in the number of clergy or ministers who apply for, or respond to, an invitation into Masonic membership? When I reflect on the difference between the situation in the 1970s and today when almost all Lodges then had a clergyman, priest or rabbi of a recognised religious body as the Chaplain and the necessity we now have to seek out some appropriate layman, a lay reader, a local preacher, deacon or known church officer for that office, then I am rather saddened. I appreciate, of course, that from the last quarter of the 20th century there has been in my own Church, a serious imbalance as those retiring have been much more numerous than the newly ordained. The Anglican decision to allow the ordination of women has meant unfortunate resignations in the ranks of the men and no doubt those numbers will increase as it seems more likely that there will be women bishops and the acceptance of 'gay' candidates. There will be fewer priests and ministers around in the foreseeable future.

There is, however, plain ignorance which the following incident illustrates. In my second parish I began a Church meeting which any member of the congregation could attend and where they might raise matters of general concern. As a 'first' I asked the local Roman Catholic priest if he would come and tell us about some of the projects and plans in which his Church, locally and world-wide, was engaged. This 60-year-old Irish priest agreed and he was heard with kindly attention. When he invited comments or questions the father of a family who had once been Plymouth Brethren and who, I knew, had doubts about my Masonic membership asked the priest: "Is it alright for a clergyman to belong to Freemasonry?" "Well," was the reply, "it all depends on whether you are a British Mason or a Continental one. You see, if you are a British Freemason there is a copy of the Bible always open at the Lodge." That seems fine to me. Now, if it was European Masonry there is no guarantee that a Bible would be there and that does not seem fine to me. So if the clergyman is British it should be all right." There was never any more questioning of my membership but I thought it was ironic that the person who could provide this information was a priest whose vow of allegiance to the Pope was such that he could not take another as a Mason. What impressed me was that he took the trouble to do what the family in the parish apparently had not. For too long the Craft has been allowed to suffer from ignorance resulting in prejudice.

What further disturbs me is why there should be a distinction made between a layman being a Mason and a clergyman. This struck home forcibly when several years ago a Methodist minister who was a much-revered Brother and also a Provincial Grand Chaplain was told that either he must resign his place in Masonry or his position as a minister. Having three young children he had no choice, but what he could not understand was why he had this ultimatum when the Treasurer of his own church who was a Provincial officer did not. As far as private activity is concerned, what is this bar that separates one priest from another or does Revelation ch. 1 v. 6 no longer apply? As Archbishop Temple so aptly put it, "Don't be too upset at what the clergy do. They only have the laity to choose from."

It surely couldn't be a problem that, as was raised in the remarks on syncretism, the clergy are too ill informed to be able to counteract what is erroneous in Masonic ceremonies or ritual? In any case, how could it be known what clergy in Lodges have to put up with unless they are involved? Could it not be seen as more desirable that clergy should be present to protect the laity from undesirable teaching? The answer to that is NO because there is no discussion of religious topics in any case and the prayers and charges, as we have seen, are able to be fully interpreted in a satisfactory way, at least for a Christian.

There remains one matter that I raise with sensitivity but also sincerity. It has to do with example and integrity. I have recently read the latest and largest book so far to do with Druidism, entitled *Blood and Mistletoe* by Ronald Hutton. In a book of some 500 pages it is almost impossible to choose a modest section to represent this comprehensive treatment. However, as Her Majesty the Queen, who is also a Patron of English and Welsh Freemasonry, and our Archbishop of Canterbury, are involved in the Order it is only fitting to have this opportunity to learn about both its past and its present. On pp. 412f. we read the following:

"in the work of Francis Pryor, one of the few current British archaeologists to range widely across (many) periods (and one of the most exciting) … he declared in 2004 that 'today … most pre-historians would accept that the religious beliefs that formed the core of Druidism had very ancient roots indeed, at least as old as Stonehenge, and probably a good deal older." Other present authors, the Aldhouse-Greens, "have attempted to relate archaeological evidence taken from the whole of European prehistory to the phenomenon that historians call shamanism … (they) employ it in a broad sense, to mean specialists who seem to communicate with a spirit world, while in a trance state, on behalf of their peoples. They claim to have found data … that would make shamanism an essential (and perhaps THE essential) component of pre-Christian religion, and the Druids feature as one aspect of it, associated with the Iron Age."

This book also points out that Druids, like others of us, have our critics: "In 1999 Beth Coombe Harris's 1930 novel *In the Grip of the Druids* was republished by an evangelical Christian company. The preface to the new edition stated that the purpose of it was explicitly to limit the influence of modern Druids, by enabling readers to perceive the essentially heinous nature of their teachings." (p. 416: Hutton's emphasis)

What it seems to me is pertinent to the theme of this book that I have been writing are the observations just recorded. If so eminent and scholarly a leader as I believe our Archbishop to be is content in his mind and conscience that he can be a member of our Church and the Druids Order, that is acceptable to me for I know he will have weighed up his responsibilities to both groups. What I cannot understand, bearing in mind the nature of this part-time interest, is why there cannot be the same understanding of those who, also having weighed up the matter, have elected to be both a priest and a Freemason. Why is there one rule for Druidism and another for Masonry? That kind of distinction puzzles but also distresses me. Is it the case that there is a double and unjust standard here? I, for my part, can see no reason for not allowing our private double memberships.

I realise that I have raised in this chapter some hard questions that touch on 'Belief and Brotherhood'. I have no doubt that there are still other relevant matters that I may have overlooked. What I hope is that I may have suggested to both Masons and our critics some fresh ways of appreciating our ceremonies and viewing our movement. Certainly if anyone wants to raise a matter or ask a question of me then I would be happy to respond. All that I have sought has been clarity about the faith of Freemasons and a reason for the faith that is in them. If I have achieved that I am content.

EPILOGUE

In 1952 a slender book of 156 pages with a yellow cover made its appearance. Published by the Regency Press, its title was *Light Invisible* and its sub-title read: 'The Freemasons' Answer to 'Darkness Visible'. Suiting the reticence about the Craft which was common at the time the author's proper name was withheld and he was referred to as 'Vindex'. The name in English would normally mean 'defender' or 'deliverer' but it could also be termed 'avenger'. It is soon evident to anyone who reads it that all three uses of the name are fitting to the treatment of the subject.

What is also evident in the book is the stance adopted by the Craft and its leaders at that time. It was in fact one year after I was myself initiated and I can therefore testify to the truth of what this author says about what he could and could not then reveal. The book appeared just two years after the publication of the first edition of *Darkness Visible* by the Revd Walton Hannah and the extract below illustrates both the restrictions complied with and the troubled, if not harsh, reaction to someone who knew no such limitations.

Vindex wrote "It is obviously impossible for me to comment, one way or the other, on the accuracy or inaccuracy of the ritual disclosures of *Darkness Visible*. I, for one, in common with the vast majority of my brothers, took my solemn obligation very seriously indeed, and not for one moment will I betray a secret trust by even hinting that an alleged disclosure might here and there reveal the true secrets. I neither confirm nor deny *Darkness Visible*. I merely despise it and hold it in utter and withering contempt as an outpouring of a diseased mind, deserving of no notice whatsoever." (op. cit. p. 128)

That the author, so restricted in what he believed he could share with an outsider, should so sharply give vent to his frustration might seem understandable but was, I confess, not quite what I was prepared for following the revelation of his calling that he produced earlier:

"Speaking as a Chaplain of the Craft, and as a clergyman of the Church of England, I can confidently assert with my whole heart that he, Fr. Hannah, completely misunderstands the underlying principles of Freemasonry from beginning to end. Hence his views are both ignorant and worthless." (p. 44) Since the views he here dismisses have not even been given the benefit of discussion, this hardly enhances his character as a minister of the gospel. And there is more.

"In this book," he continued, "I have tried above all things to be completely honest and open. Frankness and candour can hurt no one ..." and this he must have meant to exemplify in the following passionate passage: "Freemasonry, solidly founded on the Rock of Ages, the Rock of Truth eternal and divine, has indeed nothing to fear from the paltry tommy-rot spewed forth in *Darkness Visible*, but should the Church of England make herself ridiculous by 'investigating' (in plain English, snooping) or by taking any hostile steps, the reprisal might be incalculable. Freemasonry, in its broad charity, is incapable of deliberate vindictiveness, but a pitying contempt can be even more damaging ..." (p. 12) By now a little more pity and less of contempt would have benefited this Brother's image. After all, we Masons are supposed to be upholders of charity.

After these outbursts, which tell us as much about the 'defender' of our Craft as they do about what he thought of a fellow Anglican priest, it is hardly surprising to learn that there was a stern sequel. I have in my possession not only a copy of the first edition of *Darkness Visible* but the 10th edition of 1963. By now Fr. Hannah had left the Anglican Church and was writing from the Roman Catholic parish of St. Malachy in Montreal where he was now serving as a priest of that Communion.

In the foreword to this later edition he makes several very pertinent points. He urges that all the rituals should be publicly available, that no intelligent answer to his case had yet been attempted, that there had been no conclusion to the debate on Freemasonry in what was then the Anglican Church Assembly and that there were some Christian

Freemasons who were utterly sincere. This edition also carried an Appendix D which responded to the contents of *Light Invisible*.

Noting that the latter book's author was unnamed, he showed that the same had happened with letters about his book in the Press. 70% of all the mail defending the Craft was by persons not using their correct names whilst 88% of those who criticised his book identified themselves. But it is Hannah's comments on Vindex's book that really should be noted: "Obviously written in great haste and bad temper, but here and there with devastating candour, *Light Invisible*, if genuine, is extremely disquieting. It presents Freemasonry in a rather worse light from the point of view of orthodox Christianity than does *Darkness Visible*. In the rare lucid intervals between passages of scurrilous abuse and deplorably bad history, when 'Vindex' makes some attempt to come to grips with the theological argument he not only agrees with, but underlines, my main contentions. He accuses me of misrepresenting Christianity rather than Freemasonry. 'If a Christian and a Hindoo meet together in a Lodge,' maintains the author (p. 59), 'and pray together to God, it is surely axiomatic … that the Christian must acknowledge that the Hindoo's God is ultimately the same as his own.' … The passage (p. 56) where 'natural' religion is contrasted not with the supernatural, but with the unnatural, is only one of many indications, however, that the author is very nearly theologically illiterate." It will, I hope, be clear to the reader of this book how much I would be bound to disassociate myself from Vindex's views on shared prayer.

What is disturbing about *Light Invisible* is the number of 'own goals' that this fellow clergyman concedes. I note, for example, on pp. 118f that the author stresses that Masons do not belong to the Craft because of any material advantages that they may enjoy or preferential treatment which they may be given but then I read this: "Were I a Bishop or a patron of livings, I should naturally seek out Masonic incumbents, thereby ensuring that I would be preferring clergymen of tolerant and liberal views and wider spirituality. There is nothing sinister in this, for it is only sound common sense. None but the petty-minded and the failures will object. One may feel sorry for them, but it is in the interests of no one, least of all themselves, that their petty resentments should carry weight." (op. cit. pp. 118ff) Were I to believe that this truly represented the behaviour and character of fellow Freemasons I would certainly have to think again about my membership of the Craft. Fortunately, even Fr. Hannah discerns the reaction of most of the Brethren.

"It is only fair to add, however, that the average Freemason will regard *Light Invisible* as a major blunder and indiscretion. Both in its discourtesy and in its outspokenness it is far from typical of the attitude of the majority of the Brethren as I know it. But it is disquieting to find an editorial review of this damaging book in the Freemasons Magazine No. 677, ... referring to it as an 'authoritative' statement of Masonic principles."

It is many years, indeed most of my lifetime, since I first read what a fellow Anglican clergyman thought would be a satisfactory riposte to what Fr. Hannah had published. I, too, was reared in those days when silence was required about all things Masonic in the presence of outsiders. Perhaps it was again the blessing of providence that I was occupied with serving the Craft in a leadership role, in Province or Grand Lodge, until I had the time and space to reflect on the history and nature of this ancient Society of men. By then it was also providential that the Craft leaders had begun to realise that the matters that deserved reserve and privacy were actually very few indeed. The way was cleared for a new and more frank engagement with the 'popular world', which I, for my part have been privileged to make use of.

It is in this fresh and more amenable approach to anyone who sincerely and seriously wants to know the truth about this body called Freemasonry that all the books I have of late been writing have been produced. In particular I felt that there should be some exposure of the

Craft that Vindex and that generation could not bring themselves to present. But most of all I have endeavoured, not least in this present work, to be unashamed to be the named author, to present and hear the things that have bemused and worried outsiders, and to seek to answer those concerns, not with anger and rebuke but with calmness and courtesy whilst not disguising one's conviction about the right to be a faithful member of one's religion and also a practising Freemason.

It is at this point that I close my essay into *Belief and Brotherhood* with what are more measured and acceptable if surprising words by Bro. Vindex. He wrote this: "It behoves us to be cautious in estimating our achievements. We must never exaggerate or boast of our merits. We must not indulge in false and senseless self-satisfaction or conceit. We should not be carried off our feet by presumption, rash dogmatism, or foolish assertion. A sense of proportion is needed at every stage.

"It should be a warning to our own hearts, therefore, that while we claim to be heirs to much that is best in the world, while we appreciate all the accumulated learning of the ages, while we give ourselves without stint to the sacred cause of charity in the relief of sickness and distress, we should not stultify ourselves with inordinate pride or pose as super-men before the world." (*Light Invisible* pp. 144f.) May this, by the grace of God, be the legacy that he bequeaths us.

FURTHER READING

Light after Darkness, Chief Ranami Abah, Lewis Masonic, 1992.

Strange Altars, J.W. Acker, Saint Louis, Concordia Publishing House, 1959.

What They Believe – Masons, Harold J. Berry, 1999.

Workman Unashamed, Christopher Haffner, Lewis Masonic, 2005.

The Clergy and the Craft, Revd. Forrest D. Haggard, Missouri Lodge of Research, 1970.

Darkness Visible, Fr. Walton Hannah, Augustine Press, 1975.

Christian by Degrees, Fr. Walton Hannah, Augustine Press, 1984.

The Menace of Freemasonry to the Christian Faith, Revd. C. Penney Hunt, Freedom Press, 1925.

Freemasonry – A Religion? Revd. John Lawrence, Kingsway, 1987.

Christ, the Christian and Freemasonry, W. J. McK. McCormick, 1984

A Pilgrim's Path – One Man's Road to the Masonic Temple, John J. Robinson, M. Evans & Co, 1993

Catholics and Freemasonry, Dr. L. Rumble, Australian Catholic Truth Society, 1955.

Should a Christian be a Freemason? S.P.C.K., 1951